Essays on Scientific Socialism

By

Gordon McManus B.A.(Hons)

Web: http://www.globalmessenger.webs.com/
Email: essaysonscientificsocialism@gmail.com
Copyright ©2016 **Gordon McManus**

Published by Gordon McManus & Create-Space
Distributed by Amaozn.com & Create-Space e-store
Artwork by Karl Miller
Edited by Eric Johnson

ISBN-13:978-1535065023

Dedications

To:

1) LR

2 To the 'advanced workers' of the world who want to learn something new as Marx stated.

3) To my mother who has given me absolute support.

Contents

Introduction

According to Engels, Marx founded Scientific Socialism. Scientific Socialism was the revolutionary theory of the international working class up to the death of Lenin. Lenin saw his works as part of the body-knowledge of Scientific Socialism.

This 'state of affairs' changed when Stalin took over the helm of Soviet socialism from the late 1920s. Stalin, in order to justify his rule developed 'Leninism'. From this 'basis', there developed 'Stalinism'. This lasted up to Stalin's death. The aftermath of Stalin's death saw the Communist Party of the Soviet Union (CPSU) develop the 'ideology' of 'Marxism-Leninism' to justify the system that developed in the Soviet Union from Stalin onwards. 'Marxism-Leninism' came to be the dominant ideology of the international communist movement from this period onwards.

What became of Scientific Socialism? Is 'Marxism-Leninism' the 'natural' development from Scientific Socialism? These essays explore and attempt to answer the above questions.

The essay on Globalization attempts to obtain the truth of the propositional statement 'Globalization is Imperialism'. Capitalism is in its mature epoch and this propositional statement is analyzed from the viewpoint of the principles of Scientific Socialism. 'Marxism-Leninism' approaches capitalist economic, political and social life through the prism of Lenin's theory of Imperialism as being the highest stage of capitalist development. Changes within 'mature monopoly capitalism' have not been analyzed scientifically but arbitrarily subsumed under the banner of Imperialism. This is the case with 'Globalization'. For the South African Communist Party (SACP) and the Communist Party of Britain (CPB), which are representations of 'Marxism-Leninism', 'Globalization' is a phase of Imperialism and thus assert that 'Globalization' is Imperialism'. Is this correct? I discuss the proposition of these two communist parties, one from the 'North' and one from the 'South'.

The essay on the Soviet 'system' is also looked at from the viewpoint of Marx's theory of social development, of society.

The essay on the 'philosophy of socialist humanity' is an attempt to raise the system of socialism and the possible ideological, moral super-structure that aids socialist consciousness and development.

These Essays are an attempt to ascertain whether the 'approach of 'Marxism-Leninism' is scientific and in the interests of the working class. This approach these Essays show has resulted in dogmatism that can be likened to religious zealotry. This work is aimed at the working class and especially the 'advanced workers' (Lenin) who want to learn something new based on the principles of Scientific Socialism.

Essay 1 Globalization

Introduction

In order to understand 'Globalization' it is important to set the scene, so to speak. The aftermath of the Second World War saw the world divided into two social systems capitalism, on the one hand led by the United States and 'World Socialism' on the other hand led by the Soviet Union. These competing ideologies led to the emergence of what came to be coined as the 'Cold War' which the big capitalist powers embarked on.

Within the capitalist world there were changes. The United States of America (USA) became the leading capitalist power surpassing Britain. The Second World War was economically disastrous for the Imperialist powers emanating from the continent of Europe. They had to rebuild their economies on a capitalistic basis. In the 1950s there developed a radical change in European capitalism. European capitalism proceeded on the basis of capitalist economic integration. This period was the origins of the European Union. At the same time, the Imperialist powers in Europe were faced with national liberation revolutions in the colonies. The success of the national liberation revolutions put an end to the system of imperialist colonization. Capitalism had to shed its imperialist 'superstructure' (Lenin). The imperative for capitalism was co-operation and unity in the 'war' against 'World Socialism', and, specifically, the Soviet Union. This had its expression in the North Atlantic Treaty Organization (NATO) which became capitalism's major force against 'World Socialism'.

Capitalism in the 1970s was in crisis especially in Britain. Britain joined the European capitalist economic integration project, the European Economic Community. The 1980s saw the Regan-Thatcher axis restructure capitalism. the existing chains were taken off finance capital. 'Thatcherism' which involved privatization, decentralization and deregulation led to the domination by finance capital of the British capitalist economy. This policy, which became known as 'neo-liberalism' or 'financial liberalization', began to be copied by other countries which decided to restructure their capitalist economies. By the 1990s finance capital, the big banks, dominated the world capitalist economy as never before.

The success of the national liberation revolutions during this period saw the emergence of new nation states on the world stage. Some took the national democratic path based on capitalism. Others took the path of socialism. Some took the 'revolutionary democratic' path. Countries that did not support either capitalism or socialism became part of the Non-Aligned Movement.

The Soviet Union before the Second World War was the only socialist country of the world. The aftermath of the Second World War saw the emergence of 'World Socialism', of eastern European countries that took the socialist path after the defeat of fascist Germany and occupation. The system of socialism that developed was based on the 'model' in the Soviet Union. The system in the Soviet Union was the 'state monopoly' (Lenin's concept) system of socialism. The 'state monopoly' system is where social ownership of the means of production is expressed in 'state ownership'. This leads to the State becoming the dominant force in the building of socialism. There developed a socialist 'bureaucracy' led by the Communist Party to run the economy consisting of 'state industries' and 'state enterprises'. The 'co-operative' forms of property ownership played a secondary and subordinate role.

Faced with capitalist aggression, there developed the Warsaw Treaty Organization (WTO) of socialist countries led by the Soviet Union. This was an expression of 'socialist unity' against capitalism and Imperialism. The aftermath of Stalin's death led to the rejection of 'Stalinism'. There developed the ideology of 'Marxism-Leninism', which has its roots in 'Stalinism', which was used to 'justify' the 'state monopoly' system that characterized the Soviet system. In the late 1950s there developed a split in 'World Socialism'. The split was between the Communist Party of the Soviet Union and the Communist Party of China. The Sino-Soviet split led to divisions within the International Communist Movement and led to tensions. The 1950s saw the invasion of Hungary by the Soviet Union. In 1968 there was the invasion of Czechoslovakia by Soviet forces. Both events were expressions that the working class was dissatisfied, disillusioned and disenchanted with the 'state monopoly' system. Coercion was used to keep the 'state monopoly' system intact and this was an incorrect approach.

The 1970s saw 'stagnation' in the 'state monopoly' economies. The 'state monopoly' system was showing itself as not meeting the needs and wants of the working classes and the peasantry. The working class from the countries of 'World Socialism' did not benefit from the 'state monopoly' system. The period of economic 'stagnation' finally showed itself in the rise of Solidarity in Poland. From then on the state monopoly economies, especially the Soviet Union, were in crisis. Gorbachev reforms in the Soviet Union failed primarily due to the split in the Communist Party of the Soviet Union (CPSU) The Soviet Union imploded. The USSR broke up and Russia embarked on the capitalist path. 'World Socialism' imploded.

Capitalism and its ideologists crowed. Capitalism had defeated communism. Capitalism had become the dominant mode of production in the world. It is within this context that bourgeois ideologists developed the notion of 'Globalization' to signify that capitalism had changed. These reactionary bourgeois ideologists decided to rewrite the history of capitalism. The more 'intelligent' bourgeois ideologists talked about 'financialisation' of the capitalist economy and the growing trend of capitalist economic integration.

Marx, in the chapter on General Law of Capitalist Accumulation, in Capital, argued that 'monopoly' would play the decisive role in the economic life of mature capitalism. Marx sited 'monopoly' in 'centralization', one of the features of the General Law of Capitalist Accumulation. The four features of the General Law of Capitalist Accumulation are concentration, centralization, the organic composition of capital and the industrial reserve army. Marx argued that this General Law will prevail in 'mature monopoly capitalism' with 'centralization' playing the determining role.

Lenin argues thus on Imperialism:

"(1) the concentration of production and capital has developed to such a high degree that it has created monopolies which play a decisive role in economic life; (2) the merging of bank capital with industrial capital and the creation on the basis of this 'finance capital' of a financial oligarchy; (3) the export of capital as distinguished from the export of commodities acquires exceptional importance; (4) the formation of international monopolist capitalist associations which share the world amongst themselves, and (5) the territorial division of the world among the biggest capitalist powers is completed."

For Lenin, Imperialism is the highest stage of capitalism. There can be no other stage. Lenin's definition of the 'economic essence' of Imperialism was correct at the time he wrote his book.

Lenin, based on his research, in the early part of the twentieth century, argued that concentration created monopolies. Marx sites 'monopoly' in 'centralization' whereas Lenin sites 'monopolies' in 'concentration'. This difference between Marx and Lenin is not noted and discussed by 'Marxism-Leninism'. It should be noted that Lenin could not site 'monopoly' in 'centralization' because it did not prevail in capitalist economic life during his time. One should read Lenin's Notebooks on Imperialism to understand this fact. Lenin is correct about monopolies being the decisive force in economic life and that finance capital is dominant, here he agrees with Marx, however, where they differ is on the origins of 'monopoly'.

The response of 'Marxism-Leninism'

'Marxism-Leninism' rejected bourgeois ideologists' claim that capitalism had changed as expressed in the notion 'Globalization'. 'Marxism-Leninism' held to the position that capitalism is still in the stage of Imperialism and one of its constituent organization, the South African Communist Party (SACP) even argued that 'Globalization is Imperialism'.

'Marxism-Leninism' still clings to 'concentration' determining the behavior of monopolies in the twenty first century. I shall discuss this later in relation to the Communist Party of Britain (CPB).

It is within this context that I turn to analyze the position of the South African Communist Party (SACP) presented by its General Secretary, Blade Nzimande, in a Political Report to its Central Committee, in the African Communist, No. 156, First Quarter 2001, on its website in the early part of the first decade of the twenty first century. I concentrate on its 'understanding' of 'Globalization'.

For the SACP, 'Globalization' is a *term* and not a scientific concept. On this basis, the SACP argues that:

"Globalization is both an objective and subjective process. It is a logical development of a particular form of human practices – capitalism and capital accumulation."

Having made the point that Globalization is capitalism, the SACP defines 'Globalization' thus:

"...what we refer to as Globalization is a quantitative and qualitative development and growth of Imperialism."

This position is further elaborated by Jeremy Cronin, its Deputy General Secretary and theoretician, in the African Communist No. 158 when he states that 'Globalization' is:

"...present intensified and qualitatively new phase of Imperialism."

It is clear that 'Globalization' is not only capitalism; it is Imperialism and is the 'new phase' of Imperialism.

On this premise, Cronin, in his polemics with Peter Mokaba, explains the economic basis of the current phase of Imperialism:

"In regard to the current phase of Imperialism known by the term 'globalization', the SACP... believes that it has its origins in the first half of the 1970s..."

Cronin goes on to state:

"...and in a deepening crisis of profitability in the most advanced centers of capitalist accumulation in North America and Western Europe. A key symptom of this crisis of accumulation was the buildup of financial capital in Western private banks, capital that was not being invested productively in the North."

Cronin concludes:

"A temporary and partial resolution of the problem was the swathe of loans to the developing world in the second half of the 1970s and 80s...".

The origins of 'globalization', as a 'phase' of Imperialism, are for the SACP grounded in the 'crisis of profitability', 'crisis of accumulation' and the 'export of capital' or to put it in Cronin's terms, the 'swathe of loans' during the 1970s and 80s. Cronin not only 'periodises' globalization but also discuss its origins.

The SACP asserts 'Globalization is Imperialism'. The definition of the term 'globalization' through the concept 'Imperialism' shows when the SACP provides a quote of Lenin on Imperialism:

"Imperialism is capitalism at that stage of development at which the dominance of monopolies and finance capital is established, to which the export of capital has acquired pronounced importance, in which the division of the world among the international trusts has begun, in which the division of all territories of the globe among the biggest capitalist powers has being completed."

The SACP not only provides a quote from Lenin to back its position but it provides its own definition of Imperialism:

"The one defining feature of Imperialism is that of forever drawing all countries of the world into its economic orbit, but under the terms and conditions that favour the advanced capitalist countries."

This is in relation to one of its theses on 'Globalization' which states:

"Globalization is the simultaneous integration and marginalization of developing countries."

I digress slightly to give the 'understanding' of Rob Griffiths, the General Secretary of the Communist Party of Britain, when he made a speech on the matter: *"The Movement against War and Capitalist Globalization, and the Communists"*, in June 2003, published on its website. I refer, in the main, to his remarks on 'capitalist globalization':

"The process of global exploitation and concentration of economic resources is now taking place on an unprecedented scale...It is this emerging third phase of Imperialism – the first lasted until the end of World War Two and the second until the 1990s – which is labeled 'globalization...".

I return to the SACP position. What the SACP has done is to assert that 'Globalization' is Imperialism'. The SACP does not provide economic 'evidence' to back its assertion. The SACP argues that Globalization is the *"quantitative and qualitative development and growth of Imperialism"*. The SACP does not provide any economic laws to back this statement. The SACP does not provide economic laws to show that 'Globalization is Imperialism' in its Theses. The SACP does not provide the 'capitalist character' of this statement. All the SACP theoretician/s does through this Political Report is to use dialectical categories to argue that 'Globalization is Imperialism'. Marx did not use dialectical categories to show how capitalism functions. What Marx did was to discover economic laws that determined how capitalism functions. Marx's work *Capital* is an expression of the materialist approach. The

SACP analysis lacks a materialist approach. What does 'quantitative and qualitative development and growth of Imperialism' mean? This is not explained by the SACP. It is 'phrase-mongering' and pure idealistic dialectics rhetoric. What are the economic laws that determine the 'quantitative and qualitative development and growth' is not given? The SACP is *silent* on the matter.

Cronin sites the origins of 'Globalization' in the 'crisis of accumulation' and the 'swathe of loans' in the 1970 and 80s but these are not economic laws. This is not understood by Cronin and the SACP. The origins (!) of 'Globalization' must be looked at through the operations of economic laws. The SACP is clueless on the matter in the presentation of its Theses.

Let us look at this 'notion' of the SACP of 'quantitative and qualitative development and growth of Imperialism' which is what 'Globalization' is about according to their theorizing. It has no 'economic expression' through facts or laws. Is it the 'quantitatively and qualitatively development and growth' of 'capital accumulation', of monopolies, of finance capital and the financial oligarchy. If so, what law or laws prevails? The SACP is 'silent' on the matter.

The SACP talks about the 'one defining feature' of Imperialism. Lenin gives five defining features of the 'economic essence' of Imperialism. The SACP is 'redefining' Lenin's concept of Imperialism. The SACP cannot state that Imperialism has 'one defining feature'. It is incorrect on this point. Furthermore, this 'one defining feature' is at odds with the quote from Lenin that the SACP gives. What is this 'one defining feature'? It is *"forever drawing all countries to its (Imperialism) economic orbit but under the terms and conditions that favor the advanced capitalist countries"*. In other words, Imperialism 'integrates' all countries into capitalism but under 'terms and conditions that favour' the Imperialist powers. This is how I read the definition of Imperialism given by the SACP. This definition of Imperialism of the SACP leads to it developing its thesis:

"Globalization is the simultaneous integration and marginalization of developing countries."

Given that the SACP argues that 'Globalization is Imperialism' this thesis should read:

"Imperialism is the simultaneous integration and marginalization of developing countries."

The first point to note, given that the SACP is trying to 'creatively develop' Lenin's theory of Imperialism, is that its thesis is in contradiction to Lenin's definition of the 'economic essence' of Imperialism especially the 'economic *division*' by the 'international trusts'. Imperialism is not noted for 'integration'. Imperialism, on the basis of concentration, the domination of finance capital and the monopolies, and with the 'big capitalist powers', is concerned with the economic and territorial *division* of the world.

The second point to note is the category 'developing countries'. Imperialism has never been noted for having within its 'economic orbit' 'developing countries' According to Lenin, the big capitalist powers are engaged in the territorial division of the globe which means turning those territories into colonies. Furthermore, the category 'developing countries' expresses those newly independent emerging nation states that threw of the yoke of Imperialism, of Imperialist oppression, of the system of Imperialist colonization, through national liberation revolutions. In this sense, Imperialism cannot integrate and marginalize 'developing countries'. What the SACP is attempting to do is to 'subsume' the category 'developing countries' within the concept 'Imperialism'. This is incorrect.

It is important to realize the approach of the SACP. The SACP was faced with the notion of 'Globalization' developed by bourgeois ideologists who argued that capitalism had changed and rewrote the history of capitalism. The SACP designated 'Globalization' as a *term*. The SACP then argues arbitrarily that 'Globalization is Imperialism' without basing it on economic laws. Finally, the SACP argues that 'Globalization is a *phase* of Imperialism. The SACP, on this basis, develops its theses which are concerned with the 'contradictions' of 'Globalization' (read as Imperialism). It is, in essence, an explanation of what the SACP sees as 'changes' that Imperialism has undergone. In this manner, the SACP adheres to Lenin's concept of Imperialism and thus can assert that 'Globalization is Imperialism'. There is no analysis through economic laws of the changes that 'mature monopoly capitalism' has undergone in the past few decades. The SACP presentation of its Theses especially its first thesis that 'Globalization is Imperialism' is devoid of economic facts and law/s.

It is the 'Marxist-Leninist' Rob Griffiths, the General Secretary of the Communist Party of Britain (CPB) who, unwittingly, comes to the aid of the SACP and 'Marxism-Leninism'. He, too, also argues that 'Globalization' is a *term* because it does not convey 'class essence'. He argues that 'Globalization' is the third *phase* of Imperialism which began in the 1990s. Griffiths comes to the aid of the SACP and 'Marxism-Leninism' by arguing thus:

"The process of global exploitation and concentration of economic resources is now taking place on an unprecedented scale..."

Griffiths sites the 'third phase' of Imperialism which he calls 'Globalization' in 'concentration'. Arguing thus, he follows Lenin by citing the particular economic law, 'concentration' of the 'General Law of Capitalist Accumulation' as determining the 'third phase' of Imperialism.

Griffiths, in his speech, goes on to present the Communist Party of Britain (CPB) position thus:

"Our Party is critical of the term 'globalization' for three reasons,"

And they are:

"1. fails to convey the class essence;

2. it implies that capitalism has recently changed from being a national system to an international one, whereas it has been combination of the national and international from its earliest stage: national markets were formed and retain their significance in all leading capitalist countries, and state power is concentrated at the national level and used to promote each nation's capitalist class internationally;

3. Globalization is not being driven primarily by an abstract ideological commitment to the 'free market' or to a free movement of goods. The USA, European Union and Japan all operate trade barriers... None of them operates an 'open door' policy to migrant peoples."

Griffiths goes on to express his understanding of 'Globalization' thus:

"Nor do the international institutions which promote 'globalization'...WTO, IMF, World Bank, European Union, G8 summits constitute the 'international state apparatus' of an international capitalist class. In reality, they attempt to identify, balance and promote the common interests of each country's monopolies – each imperialism."

Furthermore, Griffiths goes on to argue that:

"Their policies ultimately rest on the power of the imperialist states represented in those institutions and at those summits. They do not abolish inter-monopoly and inter-imperialist conflict.

Cooperation and coordination between capitalist states does not for one minute mean that the system of state monopoly capitalism in each imperialist country has been replaced by some form of 'international state monopoly capitalism.

Even in the case of the most advanced integration of state monopoly capitalism which has been achieved – that of the European Union..."

The position of the SACP and the CPB are similar. Both view 'Globalization' as a *term*. Both view 'Globalization' as a *phase* of Imperialism. The difference between the two communist parties is that Griffiths grounds 'Globalization' in 'concentration' and that it lacks 'class essence'. For Griffiths, 'Globalization' is the 'emerging third phase' of Imperialism and is grounded in 'concentration' even though it lacks 'class essence'.

Let us first look at the 'class essence' of 'Globalization'. Griffiths and the CPB argue that 'Globalization' lacks 'class essence' but it is Griffiths who gives the 'class essence' of 'Globalization' when he states:

"Rather, so-called globalization is driven by the economic necessity of TNCs and other capitalist monopolies to maximize profits..."

The 'class essence' of 'Globalization' is capitalist profits through monopolies and other capitalist forms by exploiting the labour power of the working class. 'Globalization' is concerned with 'bourgeois interests', with the interests of monopoly capitalists. The position of the CPB and its General Secretary is confused and contradictory.

The second point to note is that both the SACP and the CPB use the word 'integration'. The category 'integration' is not a feature of the stage of Imperialism otherwise Lenin would have discussed it. Lenin argued that 'integration' was not possible because Imperialism was characterized with inter-imperialist rivalry and contradictions leading to inter-imperialist wars. For Lenin, there could not be a 'United States of Europe' because of inter-imperialist rivalry and contradictions.
Lenin argued that the stage of Imperialism is characterized by 'division': the economic division or economic partition of the world by 'international trusts' and the territorial division of the world by the biggest capitalist powers. The stage of Imperialism is characterized by 'division' not with 'integration'.

Given that 'integration' does not sit easily with Imperialism, it forms an integral part of 'Globalization'. (I shall discuss 'integration' and 'Globalization' later.) Griffiths denies, from the quotes above, 'international state monopoly capitalism'. He is incorrect. I give the views of Soviet 'Marxist-Leninists' M.N. Rydina, G.P. Chernikov, G.N. Khudokormov, in their book, *Fundamentals of Political Economy,* Progress Publishers, 1980, who argued thus:

"Imperialist integration has gained impetus since the Second World War. It is stimulated by the changed balance of power between the two opposite world systems, by the collapse of the colonial system of imperialism, and the increasing pressure for the development of productive forces on account of the scientific and technological revolution. It is influenced immensely by the growing monopolization of the capitalist economy and the development of monopoly into state-monopoly capitalism. Interstate associations are a form in which contemporary state-monopoly capitalism is developing." (p.148)

Furthermore, they argued that:

"The tendency towards the internationalization of the productive forces and the economy in general, and towards closer economic relations among nations is a progressive one. It boosts the efficiency of social labour and is conducive to the formation of the objective and subjective prerequisites for socialism." (p.138)

Soviet 'Marxism-Leninism' showed that it was more astute and erudite by talking about 'Imperialist integration' and 'international state monopoly capitalism' than Griffiths. What Soviet 'Marxism-Leninism' did was to subsume 'integration' under 'Imperialism'. They were incorrect to do so because 'integration' is not a feature of the *stage* of Imperialism.

What the Soviet 'Marxist-Leninists' did was to analyze capitalist developments in Western Europe in the second half of the twentieth century and found that 'internationalization of the productive forces' through capitalist economic integration was taking place. This was a new development in capitalism. Soviet 'Marxism Leninism' did not analyze European capitalist integration 'in and for-itself' based on economic laws but subsumed 'integration' under the 'banner' of Imperialism by developing the category 'Imperialist integration'. The category 'Imperialist integration' stands in contradiction to Lenin's theory of Imperialism. 'Integration' is not a feature or characteristic of the *stage* of Imperialism as defined by Lenin. The SACP and the CPB are following Soviet 'Marxism-Leninism' but are subsuming 'integration' under the 'banner' of Imperialism in an arbitrary way. In the case of the SACP Report, there is an absence of economic law/s to underpin their arguments. It is a characteristic of 'Marxism-Leninism' to subsume all new developments of capitalism in the past fifty years under the banner of Imperialism.

Griffiths and the CPB deny 'international state monopoly capitalism' but contradict themselves when Griffiths argues that:

"Even in the case of the most advanced integration of state monopoly capitalism which has been achieved – that of the European Union..."

Griffiths and the CPB position are confused and contradictory. I would prefer to use a British saying: that they have 'got their knickers in a twist'.

Griffiths, however, is correct to state that the European Union is 'the most advanced integration of state monopoly capitalism' even though at the same time he denies it. According to Soviet 'Marxism-Leninism' the European Union can be characterized as:

"Inter-state associations are a form in which contemporary state monopoly capitalism is developing." (Ryndina, et al, Op cit)

It should be clear that 'integration' does not sit easily within Lenin's theory of the stage of Imperialism, but modern 'Marxism-Leninism' is trying to subsume 'integration' within Lenin's theory of the stage of Imperialism and this is incorrect. Lenin's theory of the stage of Imperialism is not concerned with 'integration'. Modern 'Marxism-Leninism' is doing Lenin and the working class which they purport to represent a disservice.

The tendency to the 'internationalization of the productive forces' through capitalist economic integration is a development within capitalism and can only be analyzed through 'Globalization' and not through Imperialism.

At this juncture, it is important to understand that Griffiths talks about capitalist 'co-operation and co-ordination' but this is over-ridden by 'inter-monopoly and inter-imperialist conflict'. It means, according to Griffiths, that there does not exists 'international state monopoly capitalism' even in the case of the most 'advanced integration of state monopoly capitalism' that of the European Union. I shall discuss this later.

The response of Scientific Socialism

Introduction

It is clear that 'Marxism-Leninism' attempts to 'integrate' new developments within capitalism under the banner of Imperialism. Why is this so? Because Lenin argued that Imperialism is the highest stage of capitalism. There can be no other stage of capitalism. Is this position sustainable?

It is to Scientific Socialism as developed by Karl Marx that I turn to answer the above question.

Marx in *Capital* argues that mature capitalism would have one of the major economic laws, the General Law of Capitalist Accumulation, determining its functioning. Marx in his *Remarks on the National Question* also talks about capitalist development in its mature epoch. I give the 'understanding' of Rob Griffiths, the General Secretary of the Communist Party of Britain, published on its website in, I think, 2001:

"As far as the national question is concerned, Marx identified two conflicting tendencies in the development of capitalism: firstly, national movements are formed, led by the bourgeoisie, striving to create a national state in order to consolidate and protect a national market; secondly, capitalism tends to breakdown national barriers as trade, economic life generally, politics and culture become more 'international'. The first tendency predominates in the early period of capitalist development, while the second comes to characterize mature monopoly capitalism.

Marx regarded both tendencies as progressive, but only – especially in the case of the latter – if it did not involve the coercion of subject nationalities."

Furthermore, Griffiths points out:

"...it should be noted that Marx and Engels favoured the voluntary coming together of nationalities in bigger and more centralized states, so as to allow the fuller and faster development of the forces of production."

Griffiths shows a good 'textual' understanding of the position of Marx. When Griffiths uses the phrase 'voluntary coming together of nationalities in bigger and more centralized states', he should understand that Marx was talking that in mature capitalism countries could 'integrate'. Marx was aware that capitalist countries could engage in integration in its mature epoch. It is within this context that I turn to analyze 'Globalization'. (The criticism of the positions of the SACP and Griffiths 'understanding' is made in the chapter 'Conclusion', in the section 'Personal'.)

Globalization

Scientific Socialism provides a working definition of 'Globalization' so as to ascertain whether it is a scientific concept within Scientific Socialism or whether it is a 'term' as 'Marxism-Leninism' argues.
Scientific Socialism defines 'Globalization' thus:

"Globalization is monopoly capitalism at that stage of development in which;
(1) the General Law of Capitalist Accumulation, especially, 'centralization', prevails in economic life;
(2) leading to the dominance of finance capital, especially the financial oligarchy, and monopolies;
(3) the growing trend in the 'internationalization of the productive forces' through capitalist economic integration leading to the weakening of the nation state and national sovereignty;
(4) the deterioration in the lot of the working class,
(5) giving rise to the main contradiction of capitalism, and,
(6) the integration and marginalization of developing countries into the global capitalist economy."

Marx, in *Capital*, argues that there will be the full application of the General Law of Capitalist Accumulation through its four features or 'particulars' which are concentration, centralization, the organic composition of capital and the industrial reserve army. Marx's theory of capitalism has to show that this General Law exists in modern mature monopoly capitalism. Lenin proved one aspect of the General Law: that of 'concentration'. Scientific Socialism has to prove that the General Law prevails fully in mature monopoly capitalism otherwise Marx's theory cannot stand.

'Marxism-Leninism' in the early part of the twenty first century stills hold fast to 'concentration'. Griffiths 'concentration of economic resources' is the classical example of this approach. Why? They still adhere to 'concentration' because they have to maintain their mantra that Imperialism is the highest stage of capitalism. This makes them 'blind' to Marx's analysis of mature capitalism. They are either unaware or are ignorant that there has to be the full application of the General Law in mature monopoly capitalism for Marx to be proved correct. 'Marxism-Leninism', in this sense, treats Marx as a 'dead dog'.

Scientific Socialism argues that there is the full application of the General Law of Capitalist Accumulation in 'mature monopoly capitalism' in the twenty first century through its four features: concentration, centralization, organic composition of capital and the industrial reserve army. Lenin proved the validity of 'concentration' or 'reproduction on an extended scale'. I shall not go into it.

The organic composition of capital has two sides; the technical composition and the value composition. There is a dialectical relation between the two economic categories which affect capitalist accumulation. Monopolies pay great heed to the technical composition and how it affects the value composition. 'Globalization' brings to the fore the organic composition of capital.

There is the industrial reserve army which capitalism needs to depress wages and leads to pauperization. The European Union member states are, at present, having high rates of the industrial reserve army.

I concentrate on 'centralization'.

Introduction

I shall give, firstly, Marx's explanation of 'Centralization'. Secondly, I shall briefly look at the debate between Kautsky and Lenin on the relationship between 'centralization' and imperialism. Thirdly, I shall look at the practical realizations of 'centralization' in modern capitalist economic life of the twenty first century.

Marx's explanation of 'Centralization'

First of all, this is how Marx explains 'centralization'.

"This splitting of the total social capital into many individual capitals or the repulsion of its fractions one from another, is counteracted by their attraction. This last does not mean that simple concentration of the means of production and of the command over labour, which is identical with accumulation. It is concentration of capitals already formed, destruction of their individual independence, expropriation of capitalist-by-capitalist, transformation of many small into few large capitals. This process differs from the former in this, that it only pre-supposes a change in the distribution of capital already to hand, and functioning: its field of action is therefore not limited by the absolute growth of social wealth, by the absolute limits of accumulation. Capital grows in one place to a huge mass in a single hand, because it has in another place lost by many. This is centralization proper, as distinct from accumulation and concentration."

Marx explains what centralization is and shows the difference between 'centralisation' and 'concentration'. He, furthermore, states:

"But if the relative extension and energy of the movement towards centralization is determined, to a certain degree, by the magnitude of capitalist wealth and superiority of economic mechanism already attained, progress in centralization does not in any way depend upon a positive growth in the magnitude of social capital. And this is the specific difference between centralization and concentration, the latter being only another name for reproduction on an extended scale."

Marx makes clear that centralization, i.e., capitalist expropriating capitalist, is not dependent on concentration or 'extended reproduction'. 'Centralization' has its own laws of operation. Marx states:

"Centralization may result from a mere change in the distribution of capitals already existing, from a simple alteration in the quantitative grouping of the component parts of social capital."

Furthermore, Marx argued that:

"Centralization completes the work of accumulation by enabling industrial capitalists to extend the scale of their operations. Whether this latter result is the consequence of accumulation or centralization, whether centralization is accomplished by the violent method of annexation – when certain capitals become such preponderant centers of attraction for others that they shatter the individual cohesion of the latter and then draw the separate

fragments to themselves – or whether the fusion of a number of capitals already formed or in the process of transformation takes place by the smoother process organizing joint-stock companies – the economic effects remain the same. Everywhere the increased scale of industrial establishments is the starting point for a more comprehensive organization of the collective work of the many, for a wider development of their material forces – in other words, for the progressive transformation of isolated processes of production, carried on by customary methods, into processes of production socially combined and scientifically arranged."

Finally, Marx has this to say:

"In any given branch of industry, centralization would reach its extreme limit if all the individual capitals invested in it were fused into a single capital. In any given society the limit would be reached only when the entire social capital was united in the hands of either a single capitalist or a single capitalist company."

And,

"To-day, therefore, the force of attraction, drawing together individual capitals and the tendency to centralization are stronger than ever before."

Marx tied 'centralization' to one of the main contradictions of capitalism that he discovered. This is what he states:

"As soon as this process of transformation has sufficiently decomposed the old society from top to bottom, as soon as the labourers are turned into proletarians, their means of labour into capital, as soon as the capitalist mode of production stands on its feet, then the further socialization of labour and the further transformation of the land and other means of production into socially exploited and therefore, common means of production, as well as the further expropriation of private proprietors, takes a new form. That which is now to be expropriated is no longer the labourer working for himself, but the capitalist exploiting many labourers. This expropriation is accomplished by the action of the immanent laws of capitalistic production itself, by the centralization of capital. One capitalist always kills many. Hand in hand with this centralization, or this expropriation of many capitalist by few, develop, on an ever-extending scale, the co-operative form of the labour process, the conscious technical application of science, the methodical cultivation of the soil, the transformation of the instruments of labour into instruments of labour only usable in common, the economizing of all means of production by their use as the means of production of combined, socialized labour, the entanglement of all peoples of the world in the net of the world market, and with this, the international character of the capitalistic regime. Along with the constantly diminishing number of magnates of capital, who usurp and monopolise all advantages of this process of transformation, grows the mass of the misery, oppression, slavery, degradation, exploitation; but with this grows the revolt of the working class, a class always increasing in numbers, and disciplined, united, organized by the very mechanism of the process of capitalist production itself. The monopoly of capital becomes a fetter upon the mode of production which has sprung up and flourished along with it, and under it. Centralisation of the means of production and socialization of labour at last reach a point where they become incompatible with their capitalist integument. This integument is burst asunder. The knell of capitalist private property sounds. The expropriators are expropriated."

This, to a certain degree, is the 'essence' of Marx's explanation of 'centralization'.

The debate between Kautsky and Lenin

After Marx's death, one of his followers, Kautsky and his followers, linked 'centralization' to what Lenin called 'ultra-imperialism'. The following quote is Lenin's criticism of Kautsky and his followers' position cited in Ryndina et al in *Fundamentals of Political Economy*:

"There is no doubt that the trend of development is towards a single world trust absorbing all enterprises without exception and all states without exception. But this development proceeds in such circumstances, at such pace, through contradictions, conflicts and upheavals – not only economic but political, national, etc. – that inevitably imperialism will burst and capitalism will be transformed into its opposite long before one world trust materializes, before the 'ultra-imperialist', world-wide amalgamation of finance capitals takes place."

It can be assumed that Lenin acknowledges the 'tendency to centralization' but grounds the *revolutionary objective* in Imperialism and the particular law of concentration underpinning it. The struggle against Imperialism and the socialist transformation of society is not grounded in 'centralization' but in 'concentration by Lenin and that 'centralization' as a law did not prevail in Lenin's time.
It is clear that imperialism has not burst and capitalism has not turned into its opposite. Nevertheless, capitalism has changed since Lenin's time which has led to 'centralization' coming to the fore.

Marx talked about the 'force of attraction' and links it to the 'tendency to centralization'. He characterized capitalist behavior through centralization as 'one capitalist killing many', as capitalist expropriating capitalist/s. He argued that this showed itself through two methods: the 'violent' and the 'smoother'. How are we to read this in twenty first century monopoly capitalist economic life? In relation to the 'violent' method it is expressed though 'takeovers' in general and 'hostile takeovers' specifically. In relation to the 'smoother' method it can be seen that it is expressed in 'mergers and acquisitions'.

In the latter part of the second half of the twentieth century, mature monopoly capitalism started to engage 'centralization' as expressing the behavior of monopoly capital.

R. Went, in his book, "Globalization" (Pluto Press, 2000) has this to say:

"There is a sharp increase in international mergers and takeovers and direct foreign investment – an annual increase four times greater than the annual growth rate of international trade."

Furthermore, it is interesting to look at the view of the Sunday Times Business columnist, Irwin Stelzer, in his column (2/03/06):

"It seems that acquirers from Asia to Europe are bidding furiously for any British company with reasonable prospects. Spain Banco Santander snaps up Abbey and Ferrovial stalks BAA. Germany's Linde will swallow BOC unless the competition authorities object. Japan's Toshiba acquires Westinghouse and Nippon Glass picks off venerable Pilkington,"

Stelzer gives the following economic reason:

"The merger wave is now at levels not seen since the boom of 1999-2000. The value of announced merger and acquisitions (M&A) deals involving companies in the euro area has been running at $10 billion (£5.8 billion) per day and all global deals at about $20 billion a day...Companies that once contentedly cultivated their local and national markets are now keen to globalise their operations and tap new markets. This newest merger wave is washing across Europe, with British firms among the leading targets. It is not too difficult to see what makes British companies so enticing: they have high levels of profitability, with a return on equity of about 19%. That compares with 11% in Germany and 16% in France and the euro area as a whole...As a result of their higher profits, British companies enjoy cash flows that are mouthwateringly attractive to potential acquirers."

Stelzer, unwittingly, talks about 'attraction' in Marx's sense. It is the bourgeois ideologist Irwin Stelzer who through the use of the words 'enticing' and 'attractive' who proves Marx's economic concept of the 'force of attraction' correct. Stelzer shows that what is going on in 'mature monopoly capitalism' in the stage of Globalization is that of the capitalist expropriating capitalist through 'attraction'. Stelzer proves that Marx's particular economic law of centralization prevails in mature monopoly capitalism. This also leads to the conclusion that the General Law of Capitalist Accumulation prevails in mature monopoly capitalism in the stage of Globalization.

Takeovers, especially 'hostile' takeovers, mergers and acquisitions reflect the behavior of monopoly capital in the economic life of the twenty first century. They are 'common' to monopoly capital in the present 'historical period'. They were not 'common' in Lenin's time otherwise Lenin would have discussed it in his work on Imperialism. These economic facts of monopoly capitalism economic life cannot be sited in 'concentration' or 'reproduction on an extended scale' (Marx). They cannot be sited within the organic composition of capital, or the industrial reserve army. These economic facts can only be sited in Marx's economic concepts 'the force of attraction' and 'tendency to centralization'.

In the last decade of the twentieth century and in the first decade of the twenty first century British banks or finance capital was extensively engaged in takeovers, mergers and acquisitions. British finance capital is engaged in the process of centralization. It is bourgeois ideologists like Stelzer who prove Marx correct unintentionally.

The stage of Globalisation reflects and represents the domination of finance capital and monopolies. Before proceeding I would like to use a quote from Marx's chapter on the General Law of Capitalist Accumulation in *Capital* concerning finance capital or as he called it the 'credit system':

"...with capitalist production an altogether new force comes into play – the credit system, which in its first stages furtively creeps in as the humble assistant of accumulation, drawing into the hands of individual or associated capitalists, by invisible threads, the money resources which lie scattered, over the surface of society, in larger or smaller amounts; but it soon becomes a new and terrible weapon in the battle of competition and is finally transformed into an enormous social mechanism for the centralization of capitals."

It is clear that in Britain, for example, finance capital dominates economic life. The big banks have become an 'enormous social mechanism'. Marx ascribes to the 'credit system' the function of 'centralization of capitals'. In the last decade of the twentieth century and the first decade of the twenty first century the five big banks in Britain have become an 'enormous social mechanism' but they have also become responsible for the 'centralization of capitals'. During this period, just before the Financial Crash of 2007/8, the big banks in Britain engaged in 'centralization' whether through the 'violent' method or the 'smoother process'. The Royal Bank of Scotland took over NatWest, HSBC acquired Midlands Bank and Lloyds Bank took over TSB. It is clear that 'centralization' is reflected in the behavior of finance capital in Britain. These banks are 'global banks' and through their activities express the 'force of attraction'. Finance capital not only engages in centralization but it also 'facilitates' centralization. The 'tendency to centralization' in Britain is being halted by the competition authorities if it is not 'in the public interest'. The ruling capitalist class in Britain is fully aware of this 'tendency to centralization' and has put 'curbs' on it through, for example, the Monopolies and Mergers Commission or the Competition Authorities.

The global financial system is increasingly becoming integrated. The world financial system has three financial centers and they are Wall Street – USA, the City of London and Tokyo – Japan. Frankfurt is in the process of becoming a financial center because of the formation of the European Central Bank which expresses the 'amalgamation of finance capitals' (Lenin, cited above) in the continent of Europe because of the European Union which is an expression of capitalist economic integration.
Joseph Stiglitz, in his book, "GLOBALIZATION and its discontents", (Penguin Books, 2002) argues that it is the interests of the financial community or oligarchy, of financial capital that dominate the stage of Globalization. He states, as a former 'insider':

"The IMF is pursuing not just the objectives set out in its original mandate, of enhancing global stability and ensuring that there are funds for countries facing the threat of recession to pursue expansionary policies. It is also pursuing the interests of the financial community."

Furthermore, the IMF has gone, according to Stiglitz:

"from serving global *economic* interests to serving the interests of global *finance*."

Stiglitz explains the change in the IMF behavior thus:

"Moreover, the IMF behavior should come as no surprise: it approached the problems from perspectives and ideology of the financial community, and these were closely (though not perfectly) aligned with its interests. As we noted before, many of its key personnel came from the financial community, and many of its key personnel, having served these interests well, left to well-paying jobs in the financial community."

Stiglitz is one of the few recent bourgeois ideologists to talk about the domination of finance capital and the financial oligarchy in the stage of Globalization. Finance capital and the financial oligarchy demanded in the late 1980s and 1990s that 'financial liberalization' should be adopted by 'emerging' nation states.

It is the domination of finance capital and the monopolies that the working class is faced with. This 'domination' is expressed through the full application of the General Law of Capitalist Accumulation through its four features. Scientific Socialism argues that 'centralization' is the determining element because it represents the economic behavior of finance capital and the monopolies. Monopolies can no longer be solely grounded in 'concentration' as Lenin did in his time. This is the difference between capitalist economic life in Lenin's time and the present era of the twenty first century. Capitalism has changed in the last hundred years with economic laws that previously did not prevail in Lenin's or Marx's time coming to the fore. 'Centralization' is one of those economic laws that began to come to the fore in the late twentieth century and now is the norm in capitalist economic life, that of 'mature monopoly capitalism' in the twenty first century.

Finance capital dominance in the capitalist world cannot be questioned. In the stage of Globalization, finance capital is engaged in 'speculation'. It is engaged in making money out of money as Marx pointed out in *Capital*. The Financial Crash of 2007/8 temporarily halted the engagement of finance capital in 'speculation'. Some five years later, (in 2013) finance capital is back engaging in 'speculation'. The pre-occupation of finance capital is to make money out of money. 'Speculative' finance capital is the means by which finance capital is developing. Some bourgeois commentators call it 'casino capitalism'.

There is another side to finance monopoly capital that did not prevail within the stage of Imperialism. Lenin warned of it but it prevails in the stage of Globalization and that is *usury*. Usury capitalism, in the forms of Wonga and other pay day loans financial organizations, have developed in the last decade in Britain. It is finance capital that preys on the increasing pauperization of the working class and other working people. It is parasitic capitalism. Monopoly capitalism in the stage of Globalization cannot shed its parasitic nature because it is an exploitative system.

Britain's economy is dominated by finance capital at the cost of the 'productive economy' (CPB words) and, it, finance capital, determines the structure of the British monopoly capitalist economy. The City of London is one of the financial centers of the world. In the City of London, we see the engagement of US, European, Indian, Chinese, Japanese and other capitals. Britain does not have a motor manufacturing industry. The motor manufacturing industry is foreign owned. It is dominated by Japanese, German, French, US and Italian monopolies. Another example is the domination of the steel industry by Tata, an Indian steel monopoly. In the last twenty-five years, Britain's economy has developed through the flow of capital from foreign monopolies due to 'Foreign Direct Investments' (FDIs). The British monopoly capitalist economy can no longer be regarded as a national market dominated by indigenous monopoly capitalists. This was not the case in Lenin's time, in the heyday of Imperialism when British monopoly capitalists not only dominated in Britain but also the world. Britain has changed. Britain has lost the Empire due to the success of the national liberation revolutions. Britain is no longer the dominant economic and political power that it once was. In the last twenty-five years, since 'Thatcherism' came into being Britain has changed. 'Thatcherism' involved privatization which made finance monopoly capitalists dominant in Britain's rebalanced capitalist economy. 'Thatcherism' was about the development of 'financial liberalization' in Britain based on 'foreign direct investments'. As bourgeois politicians like to say; 'the UK is open for business'. During the boom years of 1997 to 2006 when 'New Labour' governed the country the rich got richer and the poor poorer. The rich, especially the finance monopolists, did very well until the Financial Crash of 2007/8. The Financial Crash of 2007/8 did not mean the end of the dominance of finance capital in Britain.

Capital flows out of Britain and around the globe and capital flows into Britain, into the City of London. Went, whom I have mentioned above, argues thus:

'...we are seeing an increase in the number of truly integrated global markets. For production, capital flows and trade, the world economy is increasingly one, and national markets are being replaced by global markets.'

Monopoly capitalism, especially finance capital, in the stage of Globalization, is engaged in the development of 'global markets'. The development of 'global markets' based on the 'free flow of capital' from the 'advanced capitalist countries' is not a feature of Imperialism but a feature of Globalization. In the stage of Globalization, finance monopoly capitalists in the 'advanced capitalist countries' (SACP words) demanded that 'developing countries' engage in 'financial liberalization' in the 1990s. This has led to the development of an integrated global capitalist economy, given the demise of the Soviet Union and 'World Socialism', in which finance monopoly capitalists from the 'advanced capitalist countries' dominate. The finance monopoly capitalists demanded that 'developing' or 'emerging' countries open up their economies in order to 'attract' capital. James A. Hanson ('Banking in Developing Countries in the 1990s', World Bank, November 2003) points out that such a quick transformation led to '...financial crises...in the 1990s, most notably in Mexico, East Asia, Russia and Brazil.'

Given the demise of the Soviet Union and 'World Socialism' by the early 1990s, the capitalist world, especially monopoly capitalism in the 'advanced capitalist countries', had to restructure itself and developed global markets through 'financial liberalization', and in the process integrated 'developing' countries' to the capitalist mode of production. India, which is regarded as an 'emerging' country, is experiencing high growth rates because it is engaged in developing the capitalist mode of production on national soil. Brazil is developing similarly. So is South Africa whose 'National Democratic Revolution' is based on the capitalist mode of production. China is using state capitalism and capitalism to raise the level of the productive forces. They all form a part of the global capitalist mode of production. This development which has resulted in both 'global' and 'national' markets co-existing is a new development which cannot be sited within Imperialism. It has to be sited as a feature of the *stage* of Globalization. The development of 'global markets' has meant 'financial centralization'. I have mentioned Wall Street, Tokyo and the City of London. There are other financial centers such as Hong Kong, France, Singapore and increasingly Frankfurt which houses the European Central Bank (ECB). The ECB is an expression of the 'centralization' of finance capital in Europe. It is these financial centers that dominate the global capitalist economy in the stage of Globalization.

This 'financial centralization', given the global capitalist economy' cannot be sited in Imperialism which is premised on 'concentration'. These financial centers cannot be regarded as Imperialist centers. India is not an imperialist power nor is Singapore. How are we going to site the East Asian Tigers? Their development cannot be regarded as reflecting Imperialism. The 'emergence' of these countries on the global capitalist stage cannot be analyzed through the prism of Imperialism. The 'emergence' of these countries cannot be grounded in 'imperialist globalization' or in 'globalization' as the 'third phase' or 'new phase' of Imperialism. This is the difficulty I discovered when trying to analyze new developments of capitalism through the prism of Imperialism. These countries are developing the capitalist mode of production in the stage of Globalization.

I have shown that the domination of finance capital and the monopolies is now linked to centralization. There is another side to centralization which can be seen through capitalist economic integration.

Capitalist economic integration did not prevail in Lenin's time. Lenin argued that capitalist economic integration in the form of a 'United States of Europe', for example, could not happen because of 'inter-imperialist rivalries and contradictions'.

In the 1950s Europe changed. The Treaty of Rome in 1957 declared that the big capitalist powers of Europe, France, Germany Italy and others shed their 'inter-imperialist rivalries and contradictions' and embark on the process of capitalist economic integration. It was the origins of what is presently known as the European Union. The European Union (EU) is capitalist economic integration. It is an economic union. It has gone through several stages of capitalist economic integration. From the beginnings of a customs union, through the European Economic Community (EEC) or 'Common Market' to full blown economic union with a 'euro zone area' which has a common currency.

Capitalist economic integration in Europe in the form of an economic *union* is an expression of economic 'centralization' of the forces of production. The EU as an economic union is the highest expression of economic centralization. It has taken over fifty years to develop this economic centralization. With this centralization of the productive forces in Europe through capitalist economic integration has come the increasing socialization of labour.

Capitalist economic integration is a growing trend in the stage of Globalization. A few examples of capitalist economic integration are the North America Free Trade Area (NAFTA), Association of South East Asian Nations (ASEAN), Southern African

Development Community (SADC), the economic community of West African states (ECOWAS), the African Union (AU) and the Caribbean community (CARICOM). This is leading to greater economic centralization in the capitalist world in the stage of Globalization. It is important to note at this juncture that the United States of America and the European Union are to engage in talks to form a 'free trade area' which is a form of capitalist economic integration.

Schiff (Schiff, 'Regional Integration and Development in Small States', Development Research Group, World Bank, 2001.) argues for integration of smaller states and views 'joint projects' as progressive even though this involves 'some loss of sovereignty' and advocates 'regional cooperation on public goods – such as water basins (lakes, rivers,) infrastructure… the environment can generate large benefits.'

Bi-lateral and multi-lateral agreements are becoming common place for smaller states or as the SACP calls them, 'developing countries'. These are expressions of economic integration on a capitalist basis and cannot be sited within Imperialism. They have to be sited in the stage of Globalization.

European capitalist economic integration in the form of the European Union is the most advanced form of economic integration in the world. There is another side to this economic centralization in Europe. It is political centralization. This political centralization has its expression in the European Parliament, the European Council of Ministers amongst other forms. Capitalist economic integration in Europe, resulting in economic centralization, has led to political centralization. A new form of bourgeois democracy has developed in Europe, due to capitalist economic integration resulting in economic centralization, and that is the 'supranational state'. The European 'supranational state' is a new form of political centralization. From the various nation states of Europe there has developed the European 'supranational state'. This has been due to European capitalist economic integration resulting in the 'breakdown of national barriers' (Lenin). The nation state is no longer the sole expression of political centralization within Europe. This is a new development in mature monopoly capitalism in the stage of Globalization. It is a reflection of Lenin's axiom that 'economics determines politics'.

Economic and political centralization means that the big capitalist powers of Europe like Germany, France and Italy have had to shed 'inter imperialist rivalries and contradictions' and engage in capitalist 'co-operation and co-ordination'. This is being represented and reflected in the European 'supranational state'. It does not mean the end of capitalist competition. In this sense the European Union is showing the rest of the capitalist world what it has to go through. The European Union is the classical expression of capitalist economic integration.

Political centralization within the European Union in the form of the European Parliament and other institutions such as the European Commission has affected the nation state leading to its weakening and also affecting 'national sovereignty'. In Britain, the debate is alive and kicking within the bourgeois media and politicians especially within the Conservative Party.

Since the Financial Crash of 2007/8, the European Union as an expression of economic centralization has been going through a crisis. This crisis in the European Union reflects the fact that it is characterized with uneven development. Lenin's law of uneven development is fully applicable to the European Union as an expression of economic and political centralization.

It is, however, centralization that is the main economic determinant. Marx pointed out that centralization and the socialization of labour becomes incompatible with its capitalist integument. European centralization and the socialization of labour is becoming incompatible with its capitalist integument.

The application of the General Law of Capitalist Accumulation in contemporary state monopoly capitalism in the stage of Globalization proves the validity of the Scientific Socialist principles developed by Marx. It means that monopoly capitalism cannot be tied absolutely to 'concentration' and Imperialism in its mature epoch. The General Law cannot be sited in the theory of the *stage* of Imperialism because Lenin grounded Imperialism in one particular feature and that is concentration. Secondly, there is the development of 'centralization' which is a negation of concentration. Increasingly, what Marx called the 'tendency to centralization' is playing an important role in the economic life of mature state monopoly capitalism. I have not discussed the European Union for esoteric reasons but to show that it expresses economic and political centralization which cannot be explained by the theory of Imperialism. The theory of Imperialism is *silent* on the question of 'centralization' that the European Union expresses. Earlier, I gave a quote by Lenin on 'ultra-imperialism' and the criticism of Kautsky. Imperialism has not burst and capitalism has not turned into its opposite, socialism. Centralization is proceeding at quite a pace in the economic life of mature monopoly capitalism especially concerning the European Union. By limiting developments in mature state monopoly capitalism to 'concentration' 'Marxism-Leninism' cannot scientifically theorize and educate the working class. By limiting developments in mature state monopoly capitalism to 'concentration' and Imperialism as Griffiths does, 'Marxism-Leninism' takes a 'blinkered' approach to those developments.

It is at this juncture that I turn to the 'deterioration' in the lot of the working class. Marx has this to say in the chapter on the General Law of Capitalist Accumulation:

"The greater the social wealth, the functioning capital, the extent and energy of its growth, and, therefore, also the absolute mass of the proletariat and the productiveness of its labour, the greater is the industrial reserve army...But the greater this reserve army in proportion to the active labour army, the greater is the mass of a consolidated surplus-population, whose misery is in inverse ratio to its torment of labour. The more extensive, finally, the Lazarus-layers of the working class and the industrial reserve army, the greater is official pauperism. *This is the absolute general law of capitalist accumulation.*"

Marx goes on to discuss the relative and absolute deterioration of the workers' position. Lenin talked about Poverty in two senses: (1) physical poverty and (2) social poverty.

Let us take a look at the European Union. European capitalism is in a state of crisis since the Financial Crash of 2007/8. In the last five years there has been an increase in the rate of unemployed people or the industrial reserve army within the European Union. Greece, for example, has an unemployment rate of approximately 27% which is expected to grow to 30%. Spain and Portugal have high unemployment rates especially in youth unemployment. In Spain, the unemployment rate is around 27%. Youth unemployment in Britain is about 1 million and the employment rate for all adults is around 2.2 million making the unemployment rate around 7.4%. The poorer paid layers of the working class are either on minimum wage or on 'zero-hour' contracts in Britain. The drive for 'austerity' by political representatives of British monopoly capitalism shows deterioration in the lot of working people and the unemployed. Poverty in Britain is on the increase and can be seen in the increase of those using 'food banks'. In Britain, there has been a turn to usury capitalism in the form of pay-day loan companies to make ends meet which increases the debt burden. Working people and the unemployed or the industrial reserve army is 'up to their necks' in debt which is an expression of poverty. 'Consumer debt', which is at a very high level in the UK, is an expression of the 'deterioration' of the lot of working people and the 'industrial reserve army'. According to the Labour Party in Britain, since the General Election of 2010 which introduced a coalition government of Conservatives and Liberal-Democrats, working people are £1500 poorer. The vital wants and needs of working people in general and the working class in particular cannot be met by capitalism. The coalition government in Britain argues that economic 'recovery' and 'growth' will mean that 'working people' will be better off. The only class that will benefit from the 'recovery' and 'growth' is the capitalist class not the working class. The only class not in debt and at the same time getting richer is the capitalist class.

The 'Physical' and 'social poverty that exists in the 'Lazarus-layers' of the working class shows the deterioration in its position within the epoch of monopoly capitalism in the stage of Globalization. The bourgeois political representatives in Britain are well aware of this situation but propagate the notion that growth will improve their lot. Recently, at Prime Minister Questions in the House of Commons, Parliament, David Cameron, the British Prime Minister, (16/10/2013) talked about the 'working poor' He proves Marx right. The 'working poor' are an expression of the 'Lazarus-layers' of the working class. Low pay for low skill and unskilled work means poverty for workers in this stratum of the working class. In Britain, during the rule of New Labour under Blair from 1997 to 2010, low pay was subsidized by tax credits and other 'benefits'. In the age of austerity declared by Cameron since 2010 this nexus is being broken and hence the British Prime Minister talks about the 'working poor'. This situation of the 'working poor' is endemic in the capitalist world in the stage of Globalization.

In the stage of Globalization, the deterioration in the position of the workers' is very important for the transformation to socialism. Capitalism cannot meet the vital wants of the working class in particular, working people in general and the unemployed even given the 'welfare state' which did not exist in Marx's time or Lenin's time. This means that the working class has to find an alternative economic system and that is socialism. Socialism is the system that meets the need and wants of the working class in particular and working people in general. Globalization makes this transformation imminent.

Whilst centralization of the means of production develops through the behavior of finance capital and the monopolies and through capitalist economic integration as in the European Union leading to greater social wealth in the hands of the finance capitalists and monopoly capitalists, there is also the deterioration of the position of the working class occurring at the same time. This contradiction has to be resolved.

Marx is correct in his discussion on the absolute general law of capitalist accumulation and the 'deterioration in the lot of the working class' and the stage of Globalization brings this law to the fore.

I turn to the final feature of the working definition of Globalization provided and that is the 'integration and marginalization of developing countries'. I have taken this thesis from the SACP and included it in the definition of the stage of Globalization which has been constructed, which sets it apart from the stage of Imperialism. This thesis contradicts and disproves the definition of Imperialism by Lenin provided by the SACP. For Lenin, the 'international trusts' or monopolies and the big capitalist powers are engaged in the economic and territorial *division* of the world. In Lenin's time the political category 'developing countries' did not exist in political life. This category 'developing countries' only came to the fore after countries engaged in national liberation struggles threw off the yoke of the system of Imperialist colonization. This category does not sit well within the definition of Imperialism by Lenin provided by the SACP. Neither does 'integration' and 'marginalization'. Scientific Socialism makes a contrast between the SACP thesis 'integration and marginalization of developing countries' and the definition of the **stage** of Imperialism by Lenin provided by the SACP so that there can be clarity. This is what Lenin states;

"Imperialism is capitalism at that stage of development at which the dominance of monopolies and finance capital is established, to which the export of capital as acquired pronounced importance, in which the division of the world among the international trusts has begun, in which the division of all of the territories of the globe among the biggest capital powers has being completed."

It is clear that the SACP thesis 'integration and marginalization of developing countries' stands in opposition, nay in contradiction (The SACP leadership and its theoreticians base their theses on the dialectical law, the law of contradiction, thus we get 'integration and marginalization' and 'strengthening and weakening of the nation-state', for examples. Thus they move from contradiction to contradiction. They 'love' expressing their theses through contradictions. These 'contradictions' are not based on any economic law. Marx, in Capital, Vol.1, first of all discusses the General Law of Capitalist Accumulation through its four features: concentration, centralization, organic composition of capital and the industrial reserve army. Then he goes on to discuss the main contradiction of capitalism: centralization of the means of production and the socialization of labour become incompatible with its capitalist integument. There is a difference between the 'methodology' of the SACP and Marx's dialectical method – in the chapter called 'Context' and in the section 'General' I provide Marx's own 'understanding' of his 'method' and compare it to the SACP 'approach' so that the reader can be clear. The SACP is critical of the approach of 'vulgar Marxism', yet its 'approach' puts it in that camp.) to Lenin's definition and in fact disproves it. If the SACP is correct then its thesis disproves Lenin definition. (In general the SACP theses take the standpoint of 'developing countries' based on its original thesis 'Globalization is Imperialism'.)

The SACP is correct when it states 'Globalization' is the 'integration and marginalization of developing countries' but only when Imperialism is stripped away from it. In the 1990s when Globalization began, according to Rob Griffiths, the General Secretary of the Communist Party of Britain (CPB), the 'advanced capitalist countries' (SACP words) and their finance capitalists demanded of 'developing countries' that they engage in 'financial liberalization' according to the 'intelligent' bourgeois ideologists on 'Globalization'. 'Developing countries' who adopted this policy became 'integrated' into the global capitalist economy but at the same time became 'marginalized' because 'capital accumulation' was dominated by the 'international trusts' and finance capitalists of the 'advanced capitalist countries'. 'Financial liberalization' is a policy that is grounded in the stage of Globalization not the stage of

Imperialism.

This thesis, the 'integration and marginalization of developing countries' negates the SACP original thesis that 'Globalization is Imperialism'. This is an objective fact. Scientific Socialism is aware that the SACP views 'Marxism-Leninism' as a 'living ideology' and is trying to 'creatively' develop it but all the SACP does is to subsume new developments of mature monopoly capitalism under the banner of Imperialism and shout 'Globalization is Imperialism'. It is sheer dogmatism.

The 'Marxist-Leninist' SACP thesis is very important for the definition of the *stage* of Globalization. I give the most important quotes:

"The one defining feature of imperialism is that of forever drawing all the countries of the world into its economic orbit, but under terms and conditions that favour the advanced capitalist countries at the expense of developing countries. This constitutes one of the major contradictions of globalization."

Furthermore:

"The most significant expression of this phenomenon of simultaneous integration and marginalization are the structural adjustment programmes (SAPs) imposed by the IMF and the World Bank on developing countries. In essence the prescriptions of SAPs aim at opening the developing world to the profit seeking activities of the transnational corporations through liberalization, privatization and deregulation..."

Finally,

"The faster the developing countries are integrated – opening their economies up – the deeper they are marginalized."

The SACP sees this thesis as one of the major contradictions of Globalization. The SACP is correct. The problem with the SACP position lies with its original thesis 'Globalization is Imperialism'. Given its original thesis, this contradiction is one of the major contradictions of Imperialism. This contradicts Lenin's definition of the stage of Imperialism provided by the SACP. Is this a 'creative development' of Lenin's theory of Imperialism?

It is clear that there is a contradiction in the economic relations between the 'advanced capitalist countries' and 'developing countries' in the present 'historical period' known as 'Globalization'. The problem lies with identifying this major contradiction of 'Globalization' as Imperialism.

Imperialism, according to Lenin, is characterized, among other things, by the economic and territorial *division* of the world by the 'international trusts' and the 'biggest capitalist powers'. How does the SACP characterize Imperialism with *integration* is not clear? What economic law or laws are responsible for this contradiction to arise is not made clear by the SACP? Lenin premised the stage of Imperialism on 'concentration'. It means that the SACP, as followers of Lenin, must argue that 'concentration' is responsible for this contradiction. Instead, what we get is the 'profit-seeking activities of transnational corporations'. Let us delve deeper into this 'phrase'. 'Transnational corporations' refers to monopolies. The second point to note is 'profit-seeking'. This means that the monopolies are engaged in capital accumulation through 'profit-seeking'. The SACP talks about 'Globalization' in terms of being 'capitalism and capital accumulation'. It is capitalist accumulation and has to fall under the General Law of Capitalist Accumulation through its four features: concentration, centralization, the organic composition of capital and the industrial reserve army. (the unemployed.) It is no longer a simple matter of premising this 'historical period' known as 'Globalization' on 'concentration of economic resources' as Rob Griffiths, the General Secretary of the Communist Party of Britain, does. The 'Marxist-Leninist' SACP is *silent* on what economic law underpins this contradiction when the SACP *'shouts'* to the world 'Globalization is Imperialism'.

The 'integration and marginalization of developing countries', which for the SACP is one of the major contradictions of Globalization, has to have as its ground the General Law of Capitalist Accumulation. Thus, this contradiction, which is an expression of the contradiction between the 'advanced capitalist countries' and 'developing countries', cannot be grounded in Lenin's theory of the stage of Imperialism premised on 'concentration', but has to be grounded in the full application of the General Law of Capitalist Accumulation within the stage of Globalization.

The General Law of Capitalist Accumulation shows itself in economic life, in the stage of Globalization, through the contradiction between 'advanced capitalist countries' and 'developing countries' which leads to the contradiction 'the integration and marginalization of developing countries' because 'capital accumulation' is in favour of the 'advanced capitalist countries'. This is the reason why it has been included in the definition of the *stage* of Globalization.

The SACP 'talks' of 'Globalization' being an expression of 'capitalism and capital accumulation' and it is correct. It however fails to see or is blind or ignorant of the full application of the General Law of Capitalist Accumulation through its four features; concentration, centralization, organic composition of capital and the industrial reserve army in the 'historical period' known as 'Globalization'. Why is this? It is because starting from the position or thesis 'Globalization is Imperialism', its theses are viewed through the prism of Imperialism. The SACP leadership and theoretician/s develop a myopic view to which to analyze new developments of 'mature monopoly capitalism'. The SACP 'partisan' approach to take an 'anti-imperialist approach' with regards to the 'historical period' known' as 'Globalization' leads it to analyze new developments of 'mature monopoly capitalism' from the standpoint 'Globalization is Imperialism', from the standpoint that Imperialism is the highest stage of capitalism. It does not occur to the 'Marxist-Leninist' SACP that this 'contradiction' has to have economic laws underpinning it and at the same time 'contradicts' aspects of the definition of Imperialism by Lenin which is provided by the SACP.

I have had to discuss the approach or 'method' of the SACP in relation to the contradiction 'the integration and marginalization of developing countries' because it subsumes this contradiction under the banner of Imperialism. This is because it 'believes' (SACP word) that there can be no other stage of capitalism within the epoch of mature monopoly capitalism. The dogmatism of the 'Marxist-Leninist' SACP does not allow it to analyze new developments of 'mature monopoly capitalism' based on Lenin's dictum 'concrete analysis of a concrete situation'.

A 'concrete analysis' of the 'concrete situation' known as the contradiction 'the integration and marginalization of developing countries' developed by the SACP will show that it is underpinned not only by the General Law of Capitalist Accumulation but also by Lenin's law, the 'law of uneven development'. These laws prevailing in the 'historical period' known as 'Globalization' means that mature monopoly capitalism has entered a new higher stage. These laws cannot be grounded in Lenin's definition of the stage of Imperialism premised on 'concentration'. (In the Chapter 'Conclusion' and the section 'General' I contrast the 'method' of Marx with the 'method' employed by the SACP in developing its theses if the reader is interested.)

Discussion

The positions of Marx and Lenin

It should be clear to the reader that the positions of Marx and Lenin on 'monopolies' are not the same. Marx, according to Engels, sited 'monopoly' in centralization whereas Lenin sites it in concentration or 'extended reproduction'. Lenin was aware that 'centralization' did not prevail in capitalist economic life in his time. Lenin saw that capitalist enterprises had grown big through extended reproduction or concentration and called these big companies 'monopolies'. However, this was not 'monopoly' in the sense that Marx attributed to it. I raise the question: Is Lenin correct to site 'monopolies' in concentration? Lenin goes against Engels who edited Marx's *Capital* (Vol.1). It is Engels in a footnote that makes the connection between 'centralization' and 'monopoly'.

The position of 'Marxism-Leninism'

'Marxism-Leninism' turns a blind eye to this difference between Marx and Engels on the one hand and Lenin on the other hand. 'Marxism-Leninism' has followed Lenin concerning monopolies being sited in 'concentration'. This is why Rob Griffiths, the General Secretary of the Communist Party of Britain (CPB), talks about:

"...concentration of economic resources..." (Op cit),

He fails to see the role of centralization and its connection to 'monopoly' as pointed out by Engels in his editing of Marx *Capital.* Griffiths is not only ignorant of this connection between monopoly and centralization he fails to see that 'concentration' is no longer the sole and main determinant of the behavior of monopolies in particular and capitalist accumulation in general in the present 'historical period'. By arguing thus, dogmatically following Lenin, he fails to see or is ignorant of the fact that the General Law of Capitalist Accumulation prevails in capitalist economic life in the second decade of the twenty first century. This is a major problem of 'Marxism-Leninism'. It clings, dogmatically, to the connection between concentration and 'monopoly' and to propagate that Imperialism is the highest stage of capitalism. This 'absolute' of Lenin's is clung to dogmatically and makes it blind to the 'massive changes' (SACP words) that capitalism has undergone in the last twenty-five years especially the rise of centralization. This is the reason why 'Marxism-Leninism' asserts that 'Globalization is Imperialism' and even goes on to argue that 'Globalization' is a 'phase' of Imperialism. The SACP argues thus. The CPB argues that 'Globalization' is the 'third phase of Imperialism'. Developments in mature monopoly capitalism are not analyzed on the basis of economic laws but are subsumed under the concept 'Imperialism'. When 'Marxism-Leninism' argues that 'Globalization is Imperialism' it subsumes 'Globalization' under Imperialism. 'Marxism-Leninism' is not employing materialist dialectics but is using some abstract formal logic to make its assertion. In the SACP case, it uses quotes from Lenin to justify its thesis that 'Globalization is Imperialism'

I turn to Marx's statement: "the force of attraction" and the 'tendency to centralization'. By his emphasis on 'concentration', Griffiths of the CPB fails to see, is unaware of or is ignorant of Marx's concepts. It is to Irwin Stezler to whom I am grateful because this bourgeois ideologist wrote about the 'attraction' of capital to capital. He proves Marx right. 'Marxism-

Leninism' does not talk about the 'force of attraction' because it follows Lenin in citing 'concentration'. Griffiths dogmatism, which shows in his phrase '...concentration of economic resources...', means that he treats Marx's concepts as a 'dead-dog'. The 'force of attraction' expresses itself in monopoly behavior through takeovers and mergers. This is a fact of mature monopoly capitalism in the stage of Globalization not in the preceding stage of Imperialism.

I turn to the position of the South African Communist party (SACP). I have given their position. The problem with the SACP position that 'Globalization is Imperialism' is that there are no economic laws underpinning their arguments. The SACP argument that Globalization is "quantitative and qualitative development and growth of Imperialism" has no economic laws underpinning it. Furthermore, the SACP has this to say when it characterizes 'globalization' as a 'term':

"But when we speak of globalization as being essentially a new phase of Imperialism, we are reminding ourselves that it is a process that is riven with systemic contradictions, that is based on super-exploitation, and that is simultaneously a process of development and systematic under-development."

This is very flowery dialectical rhetoric but the only problem is that there are no economic laws underpinning it. There are no economic laws or economic facts to underpin their claim that 'Globalization' is the 'new phase of Imperialism'. The SACP position lacks a materialist approach.

The SACP has this to say on Imperialism:

"The one defining feature of Imperialism is that of forever drawing all countries of the world into its economic orbit, but under terms and conditions that favour the advanced capitalist countries."

The SACP provides its own definition of Imperialism contrary to Lenin's definition, which I have given above, which has five defining features. Secondly, 'forever drawing' can be understood as 'integration' which means that Imperialism has as a feature 'integration'. Lenin gives five defining features of Imperialism and not one of them are concerned with 'integration' otherwise Lenin would have discussed it. 'Integration' is not a feature of Imperialism but it is a characteristic of the *stage* of Globalization. This is not understood by the SACP. What the SACP has done is to subsume the concept 'integration', which has assumed great importance in mature monopoly capitalism, under the banner of Imperialism.

The General Secretary of the Communist Party of Britain, Rob Griffiths, talks about 'the most advanced integration of state monopoly capitalism...' and refers to the European Union. He is correct. Where he is incorrect is he cites the European Union as a feature of Imperialism. The European Union 'as the most advanced integration' cannot be sited in the stage of Imperialism but has to be sited in the stage of Globalization because 'integration' is not a feature of Imperialism. Capitalist economic integration which leads to economic centralization through an economic union, for example, the European Union, cannot be a feature of Imperialism because Lenin argued that Imperialism was characterized by *division* of the world by the big capitalist powers and the monopolies and premised it on concentration. The 'Marxist-Leninist' SACP and the CPB are incorrect to site 'integration' under the banner of Imperialism.

I have given a speech by Rob Griffiths, the General Secretary of the Communist Party of Britain (CPB) partly on 'Globalization'. He talks about capitalist 'co-operation and co-ordination'. 'Capitalist co-operation and co-ordination' first developed when the big capitalist powers, were faced first with Soviet Russia, then the Soviet Union, and then after the Second World War with 'World Socialism'. 'Capitalist co-operation and co-ordination' became more enhanced due to capitalist economic integration on the continent of Europe. The Treaty of Paris, signed in 1951, saw the establishment of the European Coal and Steel Community with the merging of German and French monopolies. The European Union is an expression of 'capitalist co-operation and co-ordination'. In such a development the big capitalist powers have had to shed 'inter-imperialist rivalries and contradictions'. Germany, France, Britain and others who are member states of the European Union are engaged in capitalist co-operation and co-ordination in the stage of Globalization. There has not been an inter-imperialist war emanating from the continent of Europe for over sixty years due to capitalist co-operation and co-ordination based on capitalist economic integration. Finance capital and the monopolies are conducive to capitalist co-operation and co-ordination because it facilitates its dominance in the global capitalist economy. Dahl (**Communications and Culture Transformation.** Cultural diversity, Globalization and Cultural Convergence. Project presented to the European University, Barcelona. Stephan Dahl (University of Luton), June 1998. Internet) has this to say on economic co-operation and co-ordination:

"while the number of TNCs has increased immensely, the markets also experience an enormous oligopolisation, as competitors are going out of business or are merged into existing operations. Examples of this trend are numerous. Only two companies manufacture, for example, jet airplanes and one company supplies 80% of the world computers with operating systems. In areas, where there are still numerous players, joint ventures, mergers and co-operation agreements have also been the dominant paradigm of the recent years: examples include the telecom co-operations like Global One and Unisource, and of course the recent merger of Chrysler-Daimler (and Nissan's commercial vehicle unit.)"

Furthermore, he argues:

"For example, Disney has co-operation agreements with Bertelsmann, NBS and TCI, Kirch, CLT, Ufa, Canal plus and Tfi. Some even have joint channels: such as Viacom and Time-Warner with the 'Comedy Channel'...In another interesting look at the European (or active in Europe) media moguls, Berlusconi, Kirch and Murdoch, Kliensteuber points that all of them have co-operation agreements and distribution agreements...He traces, for example, that Berlusconi has joint ventures with Kirch both in Germany, France and Italy, and co-operation agreements with both Kirch and Murdoch (Kliensteuber, 1996, p.136f)"

Thus there is economic co-operation and co-ordination among European and American monopolies.
The G8 and G20 summits are an expression of capitalist 'co-operation and co-ordination' at the political level. 'Capitalist co-operation and co-ordination' is not a feature of Imperialism as defined by Lenin. It is, however a reality in the stage of Globalization. Economic co-operation and co-ordination due to capitalist economic integration like the economic union of the EU does not mean the end of capitalist competition between the big and small capitalist countries and their finance capitalist and monopolies of the EU.

Earlier, I gave Rob Griffiths, the General Secretary of the Communist Party of Britain's 'textual' understanding of Marx's 'Remarks on the National Question' and the two historical tendencies of capitalist development. I would, at this juncture, present Lenin's understanding. Lenin has this to say in his work 'Critical Remarks on the National Question':

"Developing capitalism knows two historical tendencies in the national question. The first is the awakening of national life and national movements, the struggle against all national oppression, and the creation of national states. The second is the development and growing frequency of international intercourse in every form, the breakdown of national barriers, the creation of the international unity of capital, of economic life in general, of politics. science, etc.

"Both tendencies are a universal law of capitalism. The former predominates in the beginning of its development, the latter characterizes a mature capitalism that is moving towards its transformation into socialist society..." (From the Internet)

Lenin talks about the 'unity of capital' within 'mature capitalism'. The 'creation of the international unity of capital' within 'mature monopoly capitalism' (Griffiths words) is expressed in its most advanced form, the European Union.

The political institutions of the European Union are an expression of capitalist 'co-operation and co-ordination' based on the 'unity of capital'. Capitalist economic integration has led to capitalist economic and political co-operation and co-ordination. It has led to the 'international unity of capital'.. This is a new feature of twenty first century mature monopoly capitalism, at the stage of Globalization.

It is important to point out to Rob Griffiths, the General Secretary of the Communist Party of Britain, that 'co-operation and co-ordination' (Griffiths words) between capitalist nations in Europe is an expression that 'interstate associations' (Soviet 'Marxism-Leninism' words) are a form within which contemporary state monopoly capitalism is developing. The European Union is the most advanced integration of state monopoly capitalism. The integration of state monopoly capitalism based on capitalist 'co-operation and co-ordination', on the 'unity of capital' is a new feature of mature monopoly capitalism in the stage of Globalization. The 'integration' of state monopoly capitalism is not a feature of Imperialism and cannot be sited under the banner of Imperialism. The integration of state monopoly capitalism like the European Union cannot be denied and cannot be defined as an Imperialist creation riven with inter imperialist rivalries and contradictions or as Griffiths puts it 'do not abolish inter monopoly and inter imperialist conflict'. Griffiths fails to see scientifically the 'co-operation' or the 'unity of capital' that European monopolies and finance capitalists are engaged in. The 'Marxist-Leninist' Rob Griffiths sees all new developments of monopoly capitalism in Europe through the prism of Imperialism. This is where he goes astray. He does not present a 'concrete analysis of a concrete situation' of the integration of state monopoly capitalism on the continent of Europe. Griffiths does not understand that the new development of capitalist 'co-operation and co-ordination' based on the 'unity of capital' is a negation of 'inter-imperialist conflict'. He does not understand that capitalist 'co-operation and co-ordination' as expressed in the 'international unity of capital' is more preferable than 'inter-imperialist conflict'. Griffiths and the CPB view the European Union as an 'imperialist entity' and the 'Bosses Cub' designed to serve the interests of 'European capitalists' (Lenin).

Griffiths talks about 'the most advanced integration of state monopoly capitalism' that is the

European Union and the CPB in its 52nd Congress Resolution states that the European Union is the 'creation of Western Europe big monopolies and is designed to serve their interests...' They are correct. It means that the 'big monopolies' have had to engage in 'co-operation and co-ordination' based on the 'unity of capital' in order to achieve economic union in the form of the European Union. This is a *negation* of Griffiths claim that 'globalization' and the European Union does not 'abolish inter monopoly and inter imperialist conflict'. 'Co-operation and co-ordination' among the bourgeois classes of Europe for more than fifty years since the signing of the Treaty of Rome in 1957 has resulted in the *negation* of what Griffiths call 'inter monopoly and inter imperialist conflict'. There has been no 'inter imperialist conflict' emanating from the continent of Europe during this period. During this period of capitalist economic integration leading to an economic union in the form of the European Union, Germany has emerged as the dominant power both economically and politically which she could not achieve through two World Wars in the first half of the twentieth century. There is a *qualitative difference* that has emerged between monopoly capitalist development in Lenin's time, in the heyday of Imperialism, and the present 'historical period' known as 'globalization'. In Lenin's time capitalist economic integration could not be achieved due to 'inter-imperialist rivalries and contradictions' leading to 'inter-imperialist conflict'. Thus, according to Lenin, a 'United States of Europe' could not be achieved. In the' historical period' known as 'globalization', which emerged, according to Griffiths, in the 1990s, capitalist economic integration in the form of the European Union has become a reality in the economic and political life of monopoly capitalism. This 'historical period' shows that in order for this to happen there had to be a *negation* of 'inter imperialist conflicts' and a *positive* affirmation for 'co-operation and co-ordination' based on the 'unity of capital'. Griffiths talks that 'co-operation and co-ordination' among capitalist nations does not mean the negation of, or abolishment of 'inter-monopoly and inter-imperialist conflict'. The bourgeois classes of Europe have engaged in capitalist economic *integration*, not *division* as Lenin argued, that has not seen 'inter-imperialist conflict' for the last sixty years. Two world wars emanated from the continent of Europe in the first half of the twentieth century. In the second half of the twentieth century and in the first decade of the twenty first century, there have been no wars or conflict reflecting 'inter-imperialist contradictions and rivalries' emanating from the European Union. The history of the most 'advanced integration of state monopoly capitalism' that of the European Union shows that its bourgeois classes, consisting in the main of finance capitalists and monopolists, have had to negate 'inter-imperialist conflict' and project 'co-operation and co-ordination' in order to engage in capitalist economic integration so as to increase capital accumulation and hence profits. The General Law of Capitalist Accumulation, discovered by Marx, especially 'centralization', prevails in the existence of the European Union.

Why does Griffiths argue that 'co-operation and co-ordination' does not abolish 'inter-monopoly or inter-imperialist conflict'? It is interesting to examine the approach of Griffiths. It is based on 'Globalization is Imperialism'. This is based on Lenin's absolute 'Imperialism is the highest stage of capitalism'. For Griffiths, the big Imperialist powers, Germany, France, Belgium, Britain, amongst others have formed an 'imperialist bloc', the European Union, which is strewn with 'inter-imperialist rivalries and contradictions' which lead to 'inter-monopoly and inter-imperialist conflict'. It is the 'bosses club', which serves the interests of finance capital and the big monopolies, not the interests of the British working class. This myopic and dogmatic view of the European Union, and it is nothing else but dogmatism by Griffiths, dis-colours the fact that European capitalist economic integration has brought peace to the continent of Europe including Britain for the last sixty years. Griffiths raises the 'bogey' of 'inter-monopoly and inter-imperialist conflict' in order to show his 'anti-imperialist attitude', his 'anti- imperialist credentials', to prove that he is a principled 'Marxist-Leninist'. Griffiths raises capitalist 'co-operation and co-ordination' but does not discuss it in a 'serious way' so as to educate the British working class, especially the 'advanced workers' in relation to this new development. What he does is to dismiss it on the basis that 'inter-monopoly and inter-imperialist conflict' cannot be abolished. Imperialism is the paradigm, the prism, within which Griffiths views the European Union and 'globalization' that it prevents him from analyzing scientifically the new development of capitalist 'co-operation and co-ordination' in the form of the 'international unity of capital'.

The bourgeois class of the capitalist nations is engaged in 'co-operation and co-ordination' based on the 'unity of capital' in order to perpetuate their rule, especially within the European Union. They are no longer engaged in conflict amongst themselves and thus are not able to maintain their rule. It is clear that capitalists have become more sophisticated in mature monopoly capitalism in the stage of Globalization. One of their 'unique selling points' is now democracy to the peoples of the world on the basis of capitalism. This is why they need to co-operate and co-ordinate their class interests in the stage of Globalization. The European Union is an expression of such an approach. The irony of such an approach shows itself when capitalism whilst selling 'democracy' to the peoples of the world wants to maintain its economic exploitation of the working class.

From the General Law of Capitalist Accumulation prevailing in contemporary state monopoly capitalism with centralization being the determining element leading to capitalist 'co-operation and co-ordination' shows that there have been changes in capitalism in the last twenty-five years which cannot be sited under the banner of Imperialism. Soviet 'Marxism-Leninism' talked about 'integration' and 'interstate associations' and sited it in Imperialism. Thus, we have for example, 'Imperialist integration'. 'Marxism-Leninism' in the second decade of the twenty first century has failed to view 'integration' and 'interstate associations', for example, the European Union, concretely and are following Soviet 'Marxism-Leninism'. The failure of Soviet 'Marxism-Leninism' was that it was blind to fact that 'integration' and 'interstate associations' lead to economic and political *centralization* and a loss of national sovereignty. By dogmatically following Lenin and his theory of Imperialism Soviet 'Marxism-Leninism' sited all new developments of capitalism under the banner of Imperialism. 'Centralization' was ignored and Marx treated as a 'dead dog'.

The approach of contemporary 'Marxism-Leninism' that 'Globalization is Imperialism' is a sad attempt to maintain Lenin's theory of the highest stage of Imperialism. The SACP and the CPB fail to see that their approach makes them blind to Marx's main contradiction of capitalism that centralization of the means of production and the socialization of labour becomes incompatible with its capitalist integument.

At this 'juncture' there needs to be an examination of the position of the Soviet 'Marxism-Leninism', Ryndina, et al, on the notion 'Imperialist integration' have this to say on this matter.

"The state monopoly character of modern capitalism is constantly increasing and ever greater use is being made of the state levers for stimulating monopoly concentration of production and capital...imperialist integration and new forms of capital export" (p.122-123)

Soviet 'Marxism-Leninism' tied 'monopoly concentration of production and capital to 'imperialist integration'. This is the first point to note.

Moreover, these Soviet theoreticians connected state monopoly capitalism, based on 'concentration of production and capital', to Marx's main contradiction of capitalist development:

"Under state monopoly capitalism, the socio-economic and political contradictions are further aggravated.

The first to be mentioned in this connection is the main contradiction of capitalism. Centralization of the economy on a national and international scale, while the means of production remain in private ownership, inevitably intensifies the antagonisms of capitalist society." (p.134)

These Soviet 'Marxist-Leninist' linked 'Imperialist integration' and 'capital export' to 'state monopoly capitalism' based on 'concentration of production and capital'. The weakness of their position is the linkage between 'concentration' and the main contradiction of capitalism which involves 'centralization'. This is not explained. They do not show how from 'concentration' 'centralization' arises. They are influenced by Lenin when emphasizing 'concentration'. Marx links the main contradiction of capitalism to 'centralization' and not to 'concentration' (as I have shown above) and as a 'particular' feature of the General Law of Capitalist Accumulation. Furthermore, modern state monopoly capitalism cannot be solely premised on 'concentration' as 'centralization' has come to the fore. These Soviet 'Marxist-Leninists' failed to analyze scientifically 'centralization' and how it shows itself in the economic life of state monopoly capitalism especially in relation to the then EEC. They failed to fully appreciate Marx's very important concept 'centralization'.

These Soviet 'Marxist-Leninists' 'creative' development of the main contradiction of capitalism is shown in the phrase 'Centralisation of the economy on a national and international scale...' This is an improvement. Britain, as a member-state of the European Union, has a centralized economy both on a national and international 'scale' due to economic union which is an expression of capitalist economic integration. Britain is a part of the 'centralized monolith', the European Union, as well as having an increasingly 'centralized' national economy.

These 'theoreticians' cannot be said to be ignorant of 'centralization' but they lay emphasis on 'concentration' following Lenin. They failed to understand that when they talked about the European Economic Community or the 'Common Market', as an expression of 'Imperialist integration', having an 'invigorating' effect on state monopoly capitalism in Europe in the early 1980s, that this was an expression of the 'tendency to centralization' which means the main contradiction coming to the fore. Griffiths, the General Secretary of the Communist Party of Britain, is ignorant or not aware of this connection that was developed between 'concentration' and 'centralization of the economy on a national and international scale' by Soviet 'Marxist-Leninists' when he talks about 'concentration of economic resources...'. It is his emphasis on 'concentration' that makes him blind to the main contradiction of capitalism or else it is a 'lack of theory'. (Engels)

'Marxism-Leninism' by asserting 'Globalization is Imperialism' deny bourgeois ideologists claims that capitalism has changed when the latter developed the notion 'Globalization'. The

SACP and the CPB both site 'Globalization' as a *phase* of Imperialism. Both 'Marxist-Leninist' organizations are in agreement that Imperialism is the highest stage of capitalism. This is an archaic argument and citing Lenin as an authority does not explain the changes that capitalism has undergone in the last twenty-five years. In the case of the SACP, their definition of Globalization as 'quantitative and qualitative development and growth of Imperialism' is patently incorrect. It is state monopoly capitalism that has developed and grown into a new higher stage based on the full application of Marx's General Law of Capitalist Accumulation. 'Mature monopoly capitalism' has gone through two stages. The first was Imperialism and the second present stage is Globalization. 'Marxism-Leninism' denies this reality by clinging dogmatically to Imperialism.

There has been the emergence of a European bourgeoisie (Lenin called them 'European capitalists') comprising of the bourgeoisies of the nation states of Europe due to capitalist economic integration and the 'international unity of capital'. The emergence of the European bourgeoisie is due to the breakdown of national boundaries resulting in economic union. Through economic union leading to political centralization, the European bourgeoisie is more unified than it has ever been. Lenin is correct to talk about the 'international unity of capital'. The European bourgeoisie see the value of both the nation state and the European 'supranational state' in its class interest, in its 'capital accumulation'. It is engaged in increasing 'co-operation and co-ordination' rather than engage in 'inter imperialist conflict' so that its 'capital accumulation' is enhanced.

The political representatives of the working class of the nation states of Europe who are engaged in economic union have to develop Pan-European working class co-operation and co-ordination to a very high degree to counter this growing bourgeois unity based on the 'unity of capital' in Europe. The working class political representatives of Britain and other European Union member states must see the value of working at the levels of the nation state and the European 'supranational state' in the interests of the working class. The growing trend of capitalist economic integration demands a new approach by the representatives of the working class. 'Marxism-Leninism' cannot site the struggle for socialism solely in the nation state. Economic union in Europe by the capitalist classes of the member states put paid to the old approach.

Marx remarked that the nation state is a transient form. It is not an absolute for mature monopoly capitalism. The economic and political centralization of the European Union shows clearly that the nation state is a transient form in 'mature monopoly capitalism'. The existence of the European Union, which has been the result of economic and political centralization through capitalist economic integration, has clearly shown that the nation state is not an absolute form for mature monopoly capitalism. 'Marxism-Leninism' fails to provide a scientific analysis of the relationship between the nation state and the 'supranational' state given that the European Union is a reality.

Capitalist economic integration in Europe which has led to economic union resulting in economic and political centralization has given rise to a new development in mature monopoly capitalism in the stage of Globalization and that is the relationship between the nation state and national sovereignty on the one side and the 'supranational state' on the other side. This is not an absolute opposition as there is interaction between the two that affect the interests of the working class. This relation cannot be sited under the banner of Imperialism. This new development is not a feature of Imperialism. Lenin's theory of Imperialism cannot be applied to this new development of mature monopoly capitalism within Europe. This development within Europe has meant that monopoly capital has had to shed 'inter imperialist conflict' otherwise the bourgeoisies of Europe could not unite. The new developments of mature monopoly capitalism in Europe leading to economic union and resulting in economic and political centralization based on the full application of the General Law of Capitalist Accumulation show that it has entered the stage of Globalization. Lenin's theory of Imperialism cannot explain capitalist economic integration within mature monopoly capitalism especially developments in Europe. Lenin's theory of Imperialism cannot explain the economic and political centralization that has taken place in Europe. 'Marxism-Leninism' is *silent* on this issue because it has not scientifically addressed it due to its dogmatism of clinging on to the position that Imperialism is the highest stage of capitalism. During the existence of the feudal mode of production there was first feudal *'competition'* between the barons. As the feudal mode of production developed there arose feudal *'centralization'* in the form of the monarch and the feudal aristocracy. In the stage of Imperialism there existed capitalist *'competition'* among nation states as this was the dominant expression of capitalism leading to 'inter imperialist conflict'. Within the stage of Globalization there has developed capitalist economic integration leading to capitalist *'centralization'* at the economic and political levels. The latter is clearly expressed by the European Union and other forms of capitalist economic integration. Within the stage of Globalization, capitalist 'co-operation and co-ordination' show capitalist unity or the 'unity of capital'. The European Union, an economic union, has resulted in the 'breakdown of national barriers' and has led to economic and political centralisation which reflects the second historical tendency of the 'universal law of capitalism' (Lenin) discovered by Karl Marx and discussed by Lenin. This new development cannot be sited within Lenin's theory of Imperialism and cannot be looked at through the prism of Imperialism as the SACP and the CPB do when they assert 'Globalisation is Imperialism'.

Soviet 'Marxist-Leninists', whom I have cited above, talked about 'Imperialist integration'. 'Integration' cannot be sited under the banner of Imperialism because integration is not a feature of Imperialism. These Soviet 'Marxist-Leninists' cannot argue that 'interstate associations are a form in which contemporary state monopoly capitalism is developing' and then siting it under the banner of Imperialism because 'interstate associations' are not a feature of Imperialism. Imperialism is not noted for capitalist economic integration which first developed in Europe, not noted for taking into account the resulting economic and political centralization, not noted for capitalist 'cooperation and coordination', and other new developments. These new developments are themselves a *negation* of Imperialism.

The new stage of Globalization sees the dominance of finance capital and the monopolies premised on the full application of the General Law of Capitalist Accumulation. Monopolies and finance capital are increasingly engaged in the centralization process. As the quote by Irwin Stezler proves 'the tendency to centralization' and the 'force of attraction' are important aspects in the economic life of mature monopoly capitalism. I repeat. Stezler proves Marx right. What the astute bourgeois ideologist, Stezler, sees, 'Marxism-Leninism' fails to see and thus cannot theorize scientifically about new developments that have arisen in 'mature monopoly capitalism'. The attempt of 'Marxism-Leninism' in identifying 'Globalization' as Imperialism does not educate communists and the working class in understanding scientifically contemporary state monopoly capitalism. The SACP, when it asserted 'Globalization is Imperialism' was accused of 'sloganeering' by its own cadres. Such was the paucity of their attempt to identify 'Globalization' as Imperialism. It is important to understand their approach. The SACP sees the world as Imperialist dominated by the 'advanced capitalist countries' (SACP words). On that basis they subsume all new developments of capitalism under the banner of Imperialism using formalistic methodology and language and presenting it as dialectics. I raise a question to the SACP: Are new developments of capitalism such as capitalist economic integration an aspect of the 'quantitative and qualitative development and growth of Imperialism'. As I have pointed out economic integration is not a feature of Imperialism and cannot be sited under the banner of Imperialism. Where are capitalist economic integration and its forms, like the European Union, to be sited? Capitalist economic integration exists in capitalist economic reality or life. The European Union and the United States of America are engaged in talks to form a 'free trade area' which is a form of capitalist economic integration known as the 'Transatlantic Trade and Investment Partnership' (TTIP). This new development cannot be sited within Lenin's theory of Imperialism. Contemporary mature state monopoly capitalism is engaged in economic integration rather than 'division' of the world economically and territorial by the monopolies and the big capitalist powers. This new development can only be sited in the stage of 'Globalization'.

It is clear that capitalism has changed over the last twenty-five years. These changes have gradually led to the big capitalist powers shedding' inter-imperialist rivalries' and 'conflict' and embarking on capitalist 'co-operation and co-ordination' based on the 'unity of capital'. The bourgeois ideologists who developed the notion 'Globalization' realized that capitalism was no longer in the stage of Imperialism. Their theories, which resulted in rewriting the history of capitalism, are just as poor as the SACP attempt to theorize that 'Globalization is Imperialism'.

Rob Griffiths, the General Secretary of the Communist Party of Britain, talks about 'globalization' as Imperialism and as the 'third phase' of Imperialism. He views new developments of capitalism through the prism of Imperialism and 'concentration' in order to maintain Lenin's theory. I have mentioned this before. He and the CPB have lost sight of 'centralization' in the process leading to treating Marx as a 'dead dog'. 'Marxism-Leninism' suffers from such short sightedness. Griffiths' emphasis on 'concentration' means he has to deny that 'centralization' is playing a role in the behavior of monopolies and finance capital. Griffiths approach means that he fails to see that in contemporary mature state monopoly capitalism the behavior of monopolies cannot be limited to 'concentration' but must include 'centralization' and the 'organic composition of capital'. There is the full application of the General Law of Capitalist Accumulation determining the behavior of state monopoly capitalism in the present epoch. This means that there has been a qualitative change in the *stage* that mature state monopoly capitalism is in. Lenin premised Imperialism on a 'particular' aspect of the General Law of Capitalist Accumulation, that of 'concentration'. In the last twenty-five years mature monopoly capitalism has ushered in changes which show that its behavior is determined also by centralization and the organic composition of capital. These changes have made analyzing capitalism as Imperialism redundant. Imperialism premised on 'concentration' cannot provide a comprehensive analysis of contemporary state monopoly capitalism, especially the European Union which is a form of capitalist economic integration. Capitalist economic integration and its forms are a fact of capitalist economic life. 'Concentration' cannot be used to explain the workings of capitalist economic integration and its forms. This is the problem that arose in the investigation on the matter. The workings of capitalist economic integration through its forms have to be based on centralization with concentration playing a secondary but important role. The crisis in the European Union due to the Financial Crash of 2007/8 is an expression of the fact that centralization and the socialization of labour are becoming incompatible with its capitalist integument. This is linked to uneven development within the European Union. This means that within the European Union the operation of the laws of centralization and uneven development are becoming incompatible with its capitalist integument, given the 'socialization of labour'.

'Marxism-Leninism' by emphasizing 'concentration' loses sight of the main contradiction of capitalism developed by Marx. The development of economic and political centralization resulting from the European Union as an economic union brings to the fore Marx's main contradiction of capitalism. The European Union exists and expresses Marx main contradiction of capitalism.

In looking at or analyzing the European Union as an 'Imperialist construct', 'Marxism-Leninism' and 'Marxist-Leninists' like Griffiths cannot base their analysis on centralization and linking it to Marx's main contradiction of capitalism. Griffiths cannot talk about 'Imperialist integration' because as I have mentioned 'integration' is not a feature of Imperialism. Lenin characterized Imperialism with *division.* Secondly, Lenin pointed out that 'Imperialist integration' like a 'United States of Europe' was not feasible due to 'inter-imperialist rivalries and contradictions' leading to inter-imperialist wars. Capitalism has changed. The CPB 52nd Congress Resolutions contains a section on the European Union. The CPB states that the EU is a:

'...creation of Western Europe big capitalist monopolies and has been designed to serve their interests.'

The EU is not a socialist creation. It is a capitalist creation and is not designed to propagate socialism. The EU is economic union on a capitalistic basis. It is economic centralization first and foremost and secondly political centralization on the basis of capitalism especially monopoly capitalism in Europe. The EU has been designed specifically to serve the interests of finance and monopoly capital in Europe. The CPB is correct to state that the EU is a creation of monopoly capital in Europe. Capitalist economic integration developed in Europe because it was in the interests of the monopolies and finance capital, in its striving for 'capital accumulation'.

Furthermore, and this is very important, the CPB proves Lenin wrong when the latter argued that 'international trusts' or monopolies are engaged in economic *division* of the world among themselves. The CPB, by arguing that the EU is a 'creation' of 'big capitalist monopolies' in Western Europe, show that these 'big capitalist monopolies' are engaged in capitalist economic *integration* not *division* as Lenin argued. The logical conclusion to be drawn from the CPB statement is that the 'big capitalist powers' in Europe, for example, France, Germany and others, are engaged in 'integration' not in 'dividing' the territory of Europe among themselves. It is the CPB, through its statement, that proves that the 'economic essence' (which I gave at the beginning of this essay) of the stage of Imperialism as defined by Lenin does not reflect monopoly capitalist economic life in the European Union. The CPB, through the above statement, proves that Lenin's definition of Imperialism provided by the SACP is outdated. The CPB does not realize the full import of its statement. The CPB statement, cited above, delivers a 'death-blow' to Imperialism because Imperialism is not noted for 'integration' but for 'division'. Thus, it is clear that the CPB and its General Secretary, Rob Griffiths, cannot view or argue that the EU is an imperialist construct. The CPB, if it argues that the EU is an imperialist construct, is stating that Imperialism is concerned with 'integration' and thus we have 'Imperialist integration' which was first developed by Soviet 'Marxism-Leninism' and has shown to be scientifically incorrect. The

CPB is trying to 'square the circle' when it subsumes 'integration' under the banner of Imperialism. Moreover, it is not I who proves Lenin's definition of Imperialism out-moded and outdated but the 'Marxist-Leninist' Communist Party of Britain. The CPB statement, cited above, is a correct and objective representation of the creation of the EU by European monopoly capital but in the process it contradicts Lenin's theory of Imperialism. Similarly, when the General Secretary of the CPB, Rob Griffiths, in his 2003 speech, talks about the European Union being the 'most advanced integration of state monopoly capitalism' he contradicts Lenin's theory of Imperialism which features the economic and territorial 'division' of the world by monopolies and the big capitalist powers. As I have shown 'integration' is not a feature of Imperialism and thus the EU cannot be subsumed under the banner of Imperialism but this is precisely what Griffiths does. Griffiths contradicts Lenin and at the same time he incorrectly subsumes the EU under the banner of Imperialism. The CPB is, however, unaware or is blissfully ignorant of the centralization that has resulted from economic union due to capitalist economic integration as with the EU. There is nothing on the main contradiction of capitalism as developed by Marx. The CPB approach is 'gut-hatred' for the 'Bosses Club', that is, the EU.

In order to appreciate the crass, negative approach of the noted British 'Marxist-Leninist' Rob Griffiths and his political organization, the CPB, I give the Soviet 'Marxist-Leninists' Ryndina and colleagues, whom I have cited above and repeat for convenience, who said this in 1980:

'The tendency towards the internationalization of productive forces and the economy in general and towards closer economic relations among nations is a progressive one. It boosts the efficiency of social labour and is conducive to the formation of the objective and subjective prerequisites for socialism.' (p.138)

These Soviet 'Marxist-Leninists' of yore show themselves to be more erudite than Griffiths and the CPB. The EU as an economic union of European state monopoly capitalist countries is an expression of the 'internationalization of the productive forces'. The EU is an expression of 'closer economic relations among nations'. The EU is 'conducive to the formation of the objective and subjective prerequisites for socialism'. The EU is an expression of the second historical tendency of the 'universal law of capitalism'.

Griffiths argues that Marx and Engels favoured

'...the voluntary coming together of nationalities in bigger and more centralized states, so as to allow the fuller and faster development of the forces of production'.

The European Union is an expression of the understanding of Marx and Engels. Griffiths is definitely not in tune with Marx and Engels when he calls for withdrawal from the EU. The approach of the noted British 'Marxist-Leninist' Rob Griffiths and his political organization, the CPB, is ultra-leftist and 'infantile communism' as Lenin put it.

Conclusion

I would first like to talk about bourgeois ideologists on 'Globalization'. I only used their work where relevant. These bourgeois ideologists were responsible for the introduction of the word 'Globalization' and stated that it was the new stage of capitalism. It definitely was not 'Marxism-Leninism'. These bourgeois ideologists realized that capitalism had changed in the last few decades. Their attempts to theorize on the changes led them to rewrite the history of capitalism which was crass and unbelievable. There were a few who wrote rationally and intelligently and I have used them where relevant.

It was the response of 'Marxism-Leninism' that was known to me. At this juncture I would like to tell a true story. A friend of mine, Karl Miller, came to me in 2001at a social club we both frequented and asked me these questions: what is the 'Marxist' understanding of Globalization?' What is the 'Marxist-Leninist' understanding of globalization?' I did not know the 'Marxist' understanding but I guessed and told him that the 'Marxist-Leninist' understanding is that 'Globalization is Imperialism'. I decided to do some research on the matter on the internet. I browsed the SACP website and there I found their article on 'Globalization'. I had been out of communist politics and politics in general for over ten years. I decided to do research on bourgeois ideologists positions and I browsed the websites of the World Bank, the IMF and others. One of the concepts that arose was 'integration'. Schiff, whom I have mentioned above, talks about regional integration in relation to smaller states and he was one of a few. This made me take a new look at the European Union. The research lasted four years despite a few personal mishaps. In 2005 I put together a manuscript and published it on my website www.globalmessenger.webs.com. In 2012 I came back to it and this essay is a result of my new approach.

The first concept that I was faced with was 'centralization'. In the last twenty-five years centralization has come to the fore through two sides: (1) behavior of finance capital and the monopolies, and (2) through capitalist economic integration. It meant that new developments of capitalism could not be premised on 'concentration' as Lenin's theory of Imperialism does. It meant that there was the relevancy of the General Law of Capitalist Accumulation to monopoly capitalist economic life in the twenty first century. I did not set out to prove Marx's General Law of Capitalist Accumulation. The existence and application of the General Law through its four features in monopoly capitalist economic life and I concentrate on 'centralization' shows clearly that Marx is correct about which economic law would operate in 'mature capitalism'.

The second concept that I came across in my research was 'capitalist economic integration'. This has been a growing trend within mature monopoly capitalism in the last twenty-five years. The 'classical expression' of 'capitalist economic integration' is the European Union. It is the most advanced form of capitalist economic integration in the world. Imperialism as defined by Lenin discusses the *division* of the world by the monopolies and the biggest capitalist powers. Capitalist economic *integration* and its forms are not an expression of Imperialism. Capitalist economic integration, which is a fact of capitalist economic life, cannot be grounded in Imperialism and 'concentration'. 'Marxism-Leninism' is *silent* on the matter. The closest that I got to within 'Marxism-Leninism' was when the SACP argued that Globalization is the 'integration and marginalization of developing countries'. This should read 'Imperialism is the... integration and marginalization...' because the SACP argues that 'Globalization is Imperialism'. The SACP thesis is incorrect because 'integration' is not a feature of Imperialism as defined by the quote from Lenin which they give. The use of 'integration' by the SACP contradicts Lenin's concept 'division'. What exactly is 'integration'? This is not made clear by the SACP.

'Capitalist economic integration' is a new feature of mature monopoly capitalism in the stage of Globalization. It is a *negation* of the 'division' of the world that Lenin talked about concerning Imperialism. It is not only a' negation' but is the direct *opposite* of 'division'. It cannot be sited within the theory of Imperialism. Soviet 'Marxism-Leninism' tried by talking about 'imperialist integration' and this is incorrect because it is contrary to Lenin's position. What they did was to subsume the very important concept' integration' under the banner of Imperialism. Furthermore, 'Marxism-Leninism' cannot creatively develop the theory of Imperialism by subsuming 'integration' under the banner of Imperialism on the basis of the 'quantitative and qualitative development and growth of Imperialism' as the SACP does.

The General Secretary of the Communist Party of Britain, Rob Griffiths, talks about 'concentration of economic resources'. This cannot be the sole basis for a new capitalist development like 'capitalist economic integration' in the form of the European Union, for example. The noted British 'Marxist-Leninist' is blissfully ignorant of Marx's very important concept 'centralization' because he is so *obsessed* with 'concentration' and Imperialism. By emphasizing '...concentration of economic resources...' he is ignorant that the General Law of Capitalist Accumulation prevails in 'mature monopoly capitalism' in the stage of Globalization. The General Law cannot be applied to the stage of Imperialism because Lenin sited one feature of the General Law, that of 'concentration', as the basis of Imperialism. Lenin did not cite the General Law as the premise of Imperialism. New developments in mature monopoly capitalism demand a 'concrete analysis of a concrete situation' (Lenin) not following Lenin in a dogmatic fashion.

The European Union as an economic union demands a 'concrete analysis'. The CPB is correct to point that the European Union is a creation of Western Europe monopolies but it fails to see that the monopoly capitalists of Europe are not only co-operating and coordinating their interests but are engaged in promoting economic union so as to further 'capital accumulation'. These monopolies still compete with each other but they do so, on the basis of cooperation and coordination, through an economic union. Contradictory but true. The CPB and its General Secretary fail to see that the European Union as an economic union is an expression of economic and political centralization realizing a European 'supra-national' State. With the European Union as an expression of capitalist economic integration, centralization comes to the fore.

There had to be a discussion on the European Union because it is a new development of 'mature monopoly capitalism'. There are four laws operating within the European Union. The first is the second historical tendency of the 'universal law of capitalism' discovered by Marx and discussed by Lenin. The second is the General Law of Capitalist Accumulation with centralisation being the determining element. The third is the law of the tendency of the rate of profit to decline. The fourth is Lenin's discovery, the law of uneven development within the European Union.

The new development of 'centralization', as with the European Union, brings to the fore Marx's main contradiction of capitalism. It is in the stage of Globalization that there can be seen the application of Marx's main contradiction. The European Union brings to the fore Marx's main contradiction: centralization of the means of production and the socialization of labour becomes incompatible with its capitalist integument. The existence of the European

Union and the present crisis (2013) that it is faced with shows that the centralization that it is engaged in and the socialization of labour that is developing on a great scale are becoming incompatible with its capitalist integument. 'Marxism-Leninism' in general and the Communist Party of Britain in particular are ignorant of this aspect or side of the European Union. Marx's main contradiction coming to the fore means that mature monopoly capitalism is 'moribund'. The time is approaching when the 'expropriators are expropriated'. (Marx)

Within the European Union, given the present crisis, there is the deterioration of the position of the workers. Poverty is now endemic within the 'Lazarus-layers' of the working class in Europe and the world. While mature monopoly capitalism and monopoly capitalists accrue great wealth the working class is faced with deterioration in its position. The General Law of Capitalist Accumulation can no longer be regarded as a theoretical construct but has full application in the economic life of mature monopoly capitalism in the stage of Globalization.

The General Law of Capitalist Accumulation and in particular 'centralization' must be debated by the International Communist Movement (ICM). The ICM can no longer analyze the economic life of mature monopoly capitalism solely on the basis of 'concentration of economic resources'' as Rob Griffiths does. Mature monopoly capitalism no longer functions on the basis of 'concentration'. The application of the General Law to analyze the economic life of mature monopoly capitalism necessitates a new approach. The development of this new approach means that revolutionary theory concerning the transformation to socialism will be developed. 'Marxism-Leninism', by dogmatically clinging on to 'concentration', stultifies the development of Scientific Socialism, stultifies the development of the 'advanced workers' and thus of the working class. 'Marxism-Leninism', by dogmatically clinging on to 'concentration' and 'Imperialism' neglects new developments of mature monopoly capitalism such as capitalist economic integration especially in the form of the European Union. The European Union, which is an economic union that is an expression of capitalist economic integration, which has led to economic and political centralization, only shows to the capitalist world what it has to go through. The development of the European Union cannot be premised solely on 'concentration' and 'Imperialism' but has to be premised on the full application of the General Law of Capitalist Accumulation through its four features. This is one of the conclusions reached in researching the European Union. In researching the development of the European Union, of capitalist economic integration, there was the discovery that it could not be sited within the theory of Imperialism but that it could be sited as an expression of the *stage* of Globalization.

Centralization of the means of production through the behavior of finance capital and the monopolies and through capitalist economic integration arrested the 'tendency' of the decline in the rate of profit and furthered 'capital accumulation'. The European Union, in the first decade of the twenty first century and before the present crisis, showed high rates of growth which invigorated European monopoly capitalism. Ryndina and colleagues, former Soviet 'Marxist-Leninists', whom I have mentioned above, have this to say in 1980 when Europe was at the stage of an 'economic community' or 'Common Market';

"The example of the European Economic Community makes it clear that inter-state integration can, at a certain stage, have an invigorating effect on the economic situation and the course of capitalist accumulation." (p.149)

Until the Financial Crash of 2007/8 European monopoly capitalism was doing well. Capitalist economic integration had an invigorating effect on European monopoly capitalism despite the uneven development which the present crisis has exposed. The present crisis, as I have mentioned previously, shows that centralization of the means of production and the socialization of labour in the European Union is becoming increasingly incompatible with its capitalist integument.

I have not juxtaposed concentration and centralization. I argue that the General Law of Capitalist Accumulation through its four features, concentration, centralization, organic composition of capital and the industrial reserve army determine monopoly capitalist economic life in the stage of Globalization, especially centralization. Features of mature monopoly capital like takeovers, mergers cannot be grounded in concentration or as Marx defined it 'reproduction on an extended scale' but showed their relationship to centralization and the 'force of attraction'. In the twenty first century, in the epoch of mature monopoly capitalism, monopolies cannot be grounded in 'concentration' alone as Lenin did at the beginning of the twentieth century, nearly a hundred years ago. There is also the growing trend of capitalist economic integration through forms such as customs union, free trade area, economic community and economic union. This development cannot be premised on 'concentration' and Imperialism. This development showed itself incompatible with Lenin's theory of Imperialism.

In concluding, I would like to say that I did not set out to prove Marx right and Lenin outdated. It is clear that Lenin's theory of Imperialism does not reflect monopoly capitalist economic life in the second decade of the twentieth century. I repeat the quote of Lenin provided by the SACP which I mentioned earlier:

"Imperialism is capitalism at that stage of development at which the dominance of monopolies and finance capital is established, to which the export of capital has acquired pronounced importance, in which the division of the world among the international trusts has begun, in which the division of all the territories of the globe among the biggest capitalist powers has being completed."

Does this quote of Lenin provided by the SACP reflect capitalist life in the twenty first century? Lenin talks about economic and territorial *division* of the world by the 'international trusts' and the 'biggest capitalist powers' among other things. Twenty first century mature monopoly capitalism sees the growing trend of capitalist economic *integration* in the world. Lenin's theory of Imperialism cannot account for this new development of capitalist economic integration in its classical expression, the European Union, and, in its partial expression, for example, the Southern African Development Community. The CPB position on the European Union that it is the 'creation' of Europe's big monopolies disproves Lenin's position because the big capitalist monopolies of Western Europe are engaged in economic *integration* not *division*.

The SACP argument that 'Globalization' is concerned with 'integration and marginalization of developing countries' contradicts Lenin's position. Given that the SACP asserts that 'Globalization is Imperialism', their thesis reads as 'Imperialism is the 'integration and marginalization...' which contradicts and disproves Lenin's position. Imperialism, according to Lenin's definition, provided by the SACP, is not concerned with '...integration and marginalization...' The SACP is correct in the sense that 'Globalization' can express 'integration and marginalization of developing countries' but not in the stage of Imperialism. What the SACP has done is to subsume a 'contradiction' of 'Globalization', by calling

'Globalization' a 'term' and a 'phase', under the banner of Imperialism. It is not I who disproves Lenin's theory of Imperialism but it is the SACP and the CPB who do so by trying to 'creatively develop' Lenin's theory of Imperialism whilst at the same time trying to maintain that Imperialism is the highest stage of capitalism. This is indeed a 'strange' contradiction and it is due to not applying Lenin's dictum 'concrete analysis of a concrete situation'.

The big capitalist powers in Europe are no longer concerned with the territorial division of the world or in Europe as Lenin argued. The success of the national liberation revolutions put paid to that feature of Imperialism. The new, higher stage of Globalization is concerned with the integration of 'developing countries' (SACP words) into the global capitalist system, into its 'economic orbit' (SACP words). In this sense, the SACP is correct that 'Globalization' is the 'integration and marginalization of developing countries' but where the SACP goes wrong is to identify 'Globalization' as Imperialism.

In regards to the 'export of capital', this is now a normal feature of the stage of Globalization because the 'intelligent' bourgeois ideologists talk about the 'free-flow of capital' around the world. They fail to show that it mainly emanates from the 'advanced capitalist countries'. Capital flows from the smaller capitalist powers like Singapore, South Korea and other nation-states to the 'advanced capital countries'.

All that is left from the quote of Lenin on Imperialism provided by the SACP is the 'dominance of monopolies and finance capital' and I have included this into the definition of 'Globalization' as it is still applicable at this new stage.

Both 'Marxist-Leninist' organizations, the SACP and the CPB have made statements on 'integration' concerning 'Globalization' but when they subsume these concepts under the banner of Imperialism they are engaged in 'sheer dogmatism'.

Monopoly capitalists are engaged in economic integration. Capitalist economic integration and its forms have not been discussed scientifically by 'Marxism-Leninism'. As I have mentioned Imperialism is noted for *division* not *integration*. It is the stage of Globalization that takes into account the growing trend of capitalist economic integration.

I, myself, gave a quote of Lenin on Imperialism at the beginning. I repeat the first point of the quote:

"(1) the concentration of production and capital has developed to such a high degree that it has created monopolies which play a decisive role in economic life..."

Lenin states that concentration created monopolies. In Lenin's time, 'centralization' did not prevail in the economic life of monopoly capitalism yet and thus Lenin was able to raise the 'particular' economic feature of the General Law of Capitalist Accumulation, that is, 'concentration', to the level of the 'general' and argue that it 'created monopolies'. His successors, like Robert Griffiths, the General Secretary of the Communist Party of Britain, cling to Lenin's position when they discuss monopolies in the twenty first century. I shall give a partial quote from Griffiths who says this:

"The process of global exploitation and concentration of economic resources is now taking place on an unprecedented scale..."

Griffiths sites mature monopoly capitalism in 'concentration of economic resources' and argues that Globalization is the 'third phase' of the stage of Imperialism. He follows Lenin. Scientific Socialism shows that mature monopoly capitalism is no longer governed by the particular economic law of 'concentration' as in Lenin's time. Takeovers, especially 'hostile' takeovers, mergers and acquisitions are expressions of the economic behavior of monopolies and finance capital. These expressions of monopolies behavior cannot be analyzed through concentration. Concentration or 'reproduction on an extended scale' (Marx) cannot account for these new developments of capitalism. I challenge Griffiths to prove that these new developments are expressions of 'concentration'. I could not do it. It was Stelzer who proves Marx right when the former talked about capital being 'attracted' to capital/s. What Stelzer does not have is the concept 'centralization' to base his analysis. Griffiths is completely ignorant of 'centralization' not only as an economic law but also a political concept of Scientific Socialism. Centralization has come to the fore and this is not understood by 'Marxism-Leninism' and 'Marxist-Leninists' like Griffiths of the CPB, Nzimande and Cronin of the SACP.

Griffiths may be aware of Marx's General Law of Capitalist Accumulation through concentration but his emphasis on 'concentration' has led him to ignore centralization and other features of the General Law of Capitalist Accumulation which prevail in twenty first century mature monopoly capitalism, the stage of Globalization. The existence of centralization in mature monopoly capitalist economic life of the twenty first century means that Griffiths cannot carry on emphasizing 'concentration'. His emphasis on 'concentration' leads to Griffiths, objectively, ignoring Marx main contradiction of capitalism and that is centralization of the means of production and the socialization of labour become incompatible with its capitalist integument.

Centralization, firstly through such economic forms as takeovers and mergers, and, secondly, through capitalist economic integration like the European Union, is been ignored by 'Marxism-Leninism'. On the other hand, Scientific Socialism argues that twenty first century mature monopoly capitalism is in the stage of Globalization because the General Law of Capitalist Accumulation fully prevails with centralization playing the determining role. 'Marxism-Leninism' and its individual representatives like Griffiths who cling on dogmatically to 'concentration' are not educating the working class and preparing this class for the struggle for socialism about how monopoly capital has developed through a 'concrete analysis of a concrete situation'.

New developments in 'mature monopoly capitalism' express that new economic laws have come to the fore. This is patently the case with the General Law of Capitalist Accumulation and in particular centralization. When Griffiths grounds Globalization as the 'third phase' of Imperialism based on 'concentration of economic resources', he shows that he is ignorant of the Scientific Socialist principle that new economic laws usher in a new stage of economic development. This is the case with Globalization. What Griffiths does is to subsume Globalization under the banner of Imperialism by declaring that it is the 'third phase' of Imperialism premised on 'concentration of economic resources'. That is the simple logic. Because, according to Lenin, Imperialism is the final stage of capitalism and therefore Griffiths has to ground Globalization in Imperialism. He even sees the European Union as a construct of monopoly capitalists. He is correct. Where he is incorrect is when he sees it as Imperialism. Griffiths does not understand materialist dialectical logic. Griffiths clinging on to 'concentration of economic resources' is dogmatism. He, and his party, fails to understand the significance of the Treaty of Rome when the big capitalist powers of Europe at the behest of their monopoly capitalists decided to form the European Economic Community (EEC). Capitalist economic integration like the EEC was the *negation* of 'inter-imperialist rivalry' among the big capitalist powers of Europe. These big capitalist powers of Europe when they signed the Treaty of Rome knew they had put an end to 'inter-imperialist rivalry', an end to Imperialism on the continent of Europe (at that time in the late 1950s these powers were faced with national liberation struggles which were successful and put an end to imperialist colonization) in order to engage in capitalist economic integration. The Treaty of Rome signaled, what Lenin called 'the creation of the international unity of capital'. The Treaty of Rome signified that the second historical tendency of the 'universal law of capitalism' has come to the fore. The European Union cannot be regarded as an Imperialist construct as Griffiths does because the European Union is not an expression of Imperialism. Capitalist economic integration is a new development that came into prominence in the second half of the twentieth century through Europe first and foremost. Capitalist economic integration is not a feature of Imperialism but it is a feature of the stage of Globalization.

It is important to understand that the Treaty of Rome signaled 'the creation of the international unity of capital'. Capitalist economic integration, as an expression of the 'international unity of capital', developed from the mid-twentieth century in Western Europe and has spread and is now a 'common' feature of 'mature monopoly capitalism'. The United States of America, which is the dominant finance and monopoly capitalist power in the world is engaged in a 'free trade area' in North America and is now engaged in negotiations to form 'free trade areas' with countries in the Pacific region and with the European Union. It is engaged in the 'creation of the international unity of capital'. This *objective* fact is not an expression of Imperialism but an expression of 'mature monopoly capitalism' in the stage of Globalization.

The working definition of the stage of Globalization that I gave at the beginning takes into account these new developments of capitalism. In this sense, it is a reflection of capitalist economic life in the twenty first century.

The new developments of capitalism like capitalist economic integration could not be sited within Lenin's theory of Imperialism. The full application of the General Law of Capitalist Accumulation within mature monopoly capitalism meant that mature monopoly capitalism had entered a new higher stage. That stage is the stage of Globalization.

I turned the bourgeois ideologists 'notion' of Globalization into a Scientific Socialism concept that reflects the second stage in mature monopoly capitalism. Globalization is not a 'phase' of Imperialism. 'Marxism-Leninism' has to argue that Globalization is a 'phase' of Imperialism because it follows Lenin who 'absolutely' concluded that Imperialism is the 'highest stage' of capitalism. Scientific Socialism argues and shows that Imperialism premised on 'concentration' is not the final stage of capitalism and that Globalization is not a 'phase' but the second and final stage of mature monopoly capitalism based on the full application of the General Law of Capitalist Accumulation and resulting in the main contradiction of capitalism coming to the fore. Griffiths cannot premise 'Globalization' on 'concentration of economic resources' and then argue that it is a 'phase' of Imperialism. This is 'Marxist-Leninist' dogmatism. Lenin did not talk about the 'phases' of the stage of Imperialism. 'Marxism-Leninism' has had to develop the notion of 'phases' of Imperialism in order to maintain the theory of imperialism and it being the 'final stage' of capitalism. The new developments of capitalism which Globalization expresses, firstly, are not taken into account through 'concrete analyses', and, secondly, cannot be arbitrarily subsumed under 'concentration of economic resources' as Griffiths does and then argue that it is a 'phase' of Imperialism. The new developments of 'mature monopoly capitalism' in the last twenty-five years cannot be subsumed under 'concentration' solely, like Lenin was able to do in 1916 when he wrote *Imperialism: The Highest Stage of Capitalism,* and then argued that they are a 'phase' of Imperialism as Griffiths does. Griffiths' argument that Globalization is the 'third phase' of Imperialism is 'Marxist-Leninist' dogma and not Scientific Socialist principles.

In general, Marx's method *of materialist* dialectics is concerned with how economic laws govern the behavior of 'economic agents' within a mode of production and in this case capitalism and the capitalist class. Griffiths, by grounding 'Globalization' under 'concentration' and then arguing that it is the 'third phase' of Imperialism, fails to see the working of other economic laws within mature monopoly capitalism in the twenty first century like 'centralization' which negate his approach. What Griffiths does is to elevate one particular feature of the General Law of Capitalist Accumulation, that is, 'concentration', to be the 'general' and then to argue that Globalization is the 'third phase' of Imperialism. This position is unsustainable in mature monopoly capitalist economic life in the second decade of the twenty first century. In Lenin's time, 'centralization' did not prevail in capitalist economic life, thus Lenin was able to raise the particular economic feature 'concentration' to the level of the 'general'. In Griffiths time, in the twenty first century, there is the full application of the General Law of Capitalist Accumulation and therefore Griffiths cannot raise 'concentration' to the level of the 'general' and then argue that 'Globalization' is the 'third phase' of Imperialism. In contrast, Marx and Scientific Socialism argues that the General Law of Capitalist Accumulation through its four features: concentration, centralization, the organic composition of capital and the industrial reserve army, fully prevails in the economic life of 'mature monopoly capitalism' in the second decade of the twenty first century and that Globalization is the second and final stage. Imperialism, as Lenin pointed out, was a 'special stage' but the development of mature monopoly capitalism into the stage of Globalization means that it is not the 'final stage'.

Griffiths argues that Marx and Engels were for the 'voluntary coming together' of nationalities, into bigger 'centralized' states and this needs to be discussed by the working class movement. The European Union, which as the CPB points out is a creation of Western Europe big monopolies, is that 'voluntary coming together' resulting in a bigger centralized state. Griffiths and the CPB should welcome such a development of economic union leading to political centralization, within the stage of Globalization, as Marx and Engels would have welcomed it. This development is not an expression or characteristic of the stage of Imperialism. The stage of Globalization has, as one of its features, capitalist economic integration, which means that finance capital and the big monopolies are engaged in the centralization of the means of production transcending national barriers or boundaries. It shows the coming to the fore of the second historical tendency off the 'universal law of capitalism' (Lenin). This 'centralization' which has developed from Western Europe big monopolies behavior is 'conducive' to the objective and subjective prerequisites for socialism. They do not see and thus cannot provide a scientific analysis of the European Union. Their approach is 'infantile' (Lenin) and 'leftist' because they fail to see that the European Union expresses Marx main contradiction of capitalism that centralization of the means of production and the socialization of labour is incompatible with its capitalist integument. The present crisis of European monopoly capitalism in the form of the European Union is an expression that this 'centralization' and the socialization of labour is becoming incompatible with its capitalist integument.

Capitalist economic integration, whether in the form of a custom union or economic union, is one of the last 'creations' of mature monopoly capitalism in the stage of Globalization. Mature monopoly capital cannot go back to the stage of Imperialism because it led to two world wars and numerous conflicts and in this sense 'retarded' capitalist development. Monopoly capital finds capitalist economic integration 'attractive' as it arrests the decline in the rate of profit and furthers 'capital accumulation'. During the 'boom' period, in the early years of the first decade of the twenty first century, in the stage of Globalization, the rate of profit rose in the European Union. In the 'recessionary' period of the last five years in the European Union some have called for 'ever closer union', some have called for 'reform' and some have called for withdrawal, given the decline in the rate of profit. Whichever camp wins depends on German backing which is the 'powerhouse' of the European Union. Given, this 'centralization' by monopoly capital, it is, objectively speaking, sowing the seeds of its own destruction. All it needs is a 'subjective' push. For this to happen there needs to be a scientific, conscious understanding of the working class in particular and the working people in general of the European Union and in this case, especially the 'tendency to centralization' (Marx). The May 2014 European Parliamentary election saw working people and the working class vote for the 'Far-Right' rather than the 'Left', especially, in France and Britain. Working people voted for the 'Far-Right' because of disillusionment with the European integration project and became xenophobic, nationalistic and to some extent racists. The significance of the European Union as concerning 'centralization' of the means of production, as an objective prerequisite for socialism is not discussed by Griffiths and the CPB because they regard such an approach as 'ultra-leftist'. Fighting for socialism within the European Union is for the CPB 'ultra-leftist'. Communists have to defend workers' rights that are affected by laws emanating from the European Union and this is part and parcel of the struggle for socialism. It means engaging in the European Parliament, making it fit for the purpose of defending worker's rights and to use the European Parliament to propagate worker's interests'.

The 'centralized monolith' that is the European Union must be looked at in terms of Marx's main contradiction of capitalism. It is in understanding this 'contradiction', as an 'objective' development of monopoly capital, that there can be the development of the 'subjective' factor which will fight for workers' interests both at the national and European levels. The failure of the 'Marxist-Leninist' Griffiths and the CPB to see the European Union as a 'centralized monolith' and instead view it as an Imperialist creation by Western Europe big monopolies, as the 'bosses club', as undemocratic, bows to 'workerist populism' not Scientific Socialism. In this sense, the 'essence' of 'Marxism-Leninism' is 'workerist populism'.

It is not a question of whether the European Union can be reformed or not as a recent 'Marxist-Leninist' Communist Parties communiqué (2014) on the CPB website stated. It is not a question of whether the European Union can be reformed as argued by some British and other bourgeois politicians stating their case. It is a question for communists to realize what the 'centralized monolith', the European Union, expresses. The European Union is showing that that as it develops with ever increasing 'centralization' and with the socialization of labour this is becoming incompatible with its capitalist integument. 'Marxism-Leninism' is blind to this 'tendency to centralization' and the main contradiction that Marx talked about.

Monopoly capital in Europe, which is engaged in capitalist economic integration resulting in the 'creation' of the European Union, which is a form of economic and political 'centralization', thus prepares, objectively, the path to socialism because this ever increasing 'centralization' becomes incompatible with its capitalist integument. The working people voted in Britain and France in the May 2014 European election for the 'Far-Right' in the forms of UKIP and the National Front. This demonstrates and shows the French and British workers disillusionment with the 'centralization' that the European Union is engaged in. It is the failure of 'Marxism-Leninism' to explain this 'centralization' and its consequences that led to working people in general and the working class in particular turning to the 'Far-Right' parties. It does not matter whether there was a small turnout for these elections the question is: why did working people turn to the 'Far-Right' and not vote for the 'Left'.

This 'centralized monolith', the European Union, cannot be sited or explained through Lenin's theory of Imperialism but through the stage of Globalization based on the full application of the General Law of Capitalist Accumulation through its four features especially 'centralization'. Scientific Socialism views the importance of 'centralization' in the epoch of mature monopoly capitalism as paving the way for socialism. Scientific Socialism sees 'centralization' as expressed in its most advanced form, the European Union, as an 'objective' prerequisite in the transition to socialism within the stage of Globalization.

There is increasing deterioration in the lot of the working class within the stage of Globalization. The British Prime Minister Cameron's, notion of the 'working poor' is turned into a Scientific Socialist concept because of the iron working out of the 'absolute general law of capitalist accumulation' within the stage of Globalization. In Britain, the working class is so poorly paid by the capitalist class that the taxes that it pays are used to subsidize its income through tax credits and other benefits. Marx is correct in his appraisal of how mature capitalism develops.

Bourgeois ideologists argue that capitalism is in the stage of 'Globalization'. They are correct in their 'gut-reaction' but they do not provide a scientific analysis of 'Globalization' based on economic laws. Scientific Socialism agrees with these bourgeois ideologists that mature monopoly capitalism is in the stage of 'Globalization' but differs from them in that it provides a scientific analysis of 'Globalization' based on the determination of economic laws and specifically the General Law of Capitalist Accumulation.

'Globalization' is a Scientific Socialism *concept* and expresses the second and higher stage of 'mature monopoly capitalism'. 'Marxism-Leninism's' attempt to argue that 'Globalization' is a 'term', especially in the case of the SACP and the CPB, is incorrect. No scientific proof is provided that 'Globalization' is a 'term' by the SACP or the CPB. The only 'rationale' to call 'Globalization' as a 'term', is, firstly, to deny that it is the new higher stage of 'mature monopoly capitalism', and, secondly, to subsume it under the banner of Imperialism because for 'Marxism-Leninism' Imperialism is the highest stage of capitalism. There can be no other stage. This is how 'Marxism-Leninism' and 'Marxist-Leninist' organizations like the SACP and the CPB countered those bourgeois ideologists who argued that 'Globalization' is the new stage of capitalism.

For Scientific Socialism, 'Globalization' is not a 'term', nor is it a 'phase' of Imperialism. For Scientific Socialism, 'Globalization' is a scientific *concept*, reflecting and representing developments in 'mature monopoly capitalism' in the twenty first century. For Scientific Socialism, 'Globalization' is the new, second and final stage of mature monopoly capitalism in which the General Law of Capitalist Accumulation prevails in economic life with centralization being the determining element, where there is the dominance of finance capital and the monopolies, where there is the growing trend of capitalist economic integration leading to the weakening of the nation state, resulting in the deterioration in the lot of the working class and the industrial reserve army, and, the integration and marginalization of developing countries. This brings to the fore Marx's main contradiction of capitalism that centralization of the means of production and the socialization of labour become incompatible with its capitalist integument. There needs to be developed 'revolutionary theory' that reflects mature monopoly capitalism in the stage of Globalization.

Essay 2: State monopoly system of the USSR

Introduction

I begin with a quote from Karl Marx. He discusses the proletarian revolutions of the nineteenth century. This is what he says in *The Eighteenth Brumaire of Louis Bonaparte*:

".... proletarian revolutions, like those of the nineteenth century, criticize themselves constantly, interrupt themselves continuously in their own course, come back to the apparently accomplished in order to begin it afresh, deride with unmerciful thoroughness the inadequacies, weaknesses and paltriness of their first attempts." (Marx/Engels, Selected Works, London 1968, pp.97-98)

Marx discusses the attitudes and behaviour of those engaged in proletarian revolutions in the nineteenth century with which he was well-conversed in. The most important is the dialectical approach through criticism and self-criticism and not to be satisfied with what they were creating in the name of socialism.

This was a thoroughly dialectical approach towards the new form of social development.

In the twentieth century, we saw the birth of the Great October Socialist Revolution, led by Lenin. Soviet Russia was the first country in the world to embark on the socialist path of development. It spawned other socialist revolutions in the twentieth century. China, Vietnam and Cuba are those socialist developments in the twenty first century that have their roots in the twentieth century and in the Great October Revolution.

Soviet Russia which became the Union of Soviet Socialist Republics (USSR), developed the category of 'World Socialism' as countries which gained their national liberation from fascism embarked on the path of socialist development in the post-Second World War. These countries that followed the socialist path of development based that development on the Soviet 'model'.

It is important that the lessons to be learnt from the Soviet experience are reapplied to socialist practice. There must be a dialectical approach to the failures of 'World Socialism' led by the Soviet Union so that the consciousness of workers can be scientific.

The Soviet 'model' of socialist development.

Introduction

I discuss in this chapter the 'system' of socialism that the Soviet Union, led by the 'Marxist-Leninist' Communist Party of the Soviet Union (CPSU), developed for itself after the death of Lenin. I am concerned with the socio-economic system that prevailed in the Soviet Union at the peak of its development, its classical expression, so to speak.

I first look at property ownership that existed in the Soviet Union. I, then, look at the role of the State as a means of determining the economic system that prevailed within Soviet socialism. I end by discussing the implications of such a system for socialist development.

Property forms in the USSR.

In order to understand the property form in the USSR, I give the CPSU leading theoreticians' views on the matter:

"Under socialism, social ownership of the means of production predominates. It reflects the relations between members of society, i.e., the working people in the joint appropriation of the means of production...Working people are the joint, collective masters of the material conditions of production. They form an association of workers who are free from exploitation, for they themselves own the means of production and this fact has abolished the exploitation of wage labour." (Ryndina, Chernikov, and Khudokormov, Fundamentals of Political Economy, Progress Publishers, Moscow, 1980, p.219)

It is clear from the above quote that property ownership is social under socialism. Working people own the means of production. It is this historical fact that makes property social under socialism. The Soviet Union was characterized with such a property form.

Ryndina *et al*, argue that there are two forms of social ownership of the means of production. They state:

"Social ownership of the means of production under socialism exists in two forms, viz., state (national) and collective farm and co-operative (collective-group) property." (ibid. p.220)

These authors state that 'state ownership' is the most advanced form. This is their reason:

"The leading and determining role in the system of relations of ownership and the production relations of socialism in general and in the development of the socialist national economy belongs to state ownership of the means of production. This is the determining factor that makes the entire national economy a single production mechanism, a single giant enterprise. It accounts for the prevailing part of all the means of production. These are state enterprises, with their productive capital, in all sectors of the economy, transport, banking, the land, subsoil, waters and forests ...... state ownership of the means of production is the main source of the progressive development of the national economy towards communism ..."

This was the dominant expression of property ownership in the epoch of 'developed socialism'. State property came to be the expression of property relations or ownership in the USSR. Soviet 'Marxism-Leninism' saw this as the highest and most advanced form of property relations within 'developed socialism'.

The role of the Socialist State

It is on the above property relations, that is, 'state ownership' that they discuss the economic role of the Socialist State. This is what they state:

"The socialist state led and guided by the Marxist-Leninist party is the body that controls social production under socialism... ...

Under socialism, the state controls social production by relying on the domination of national socialist property, on its leading and determining role in the country's economic development. In the Soviet Union the state owns 90per cent of all the means of production. The socialist state combines centralized guidance through instructions with economic incentives to economic growth... Being a state of the working people, the socialist state performs its economic role in their interests. This is typically both of the state of the dictatorship of the proletariat and that of the whole people, which it becomes at the stage of developed socialism.

The economic activities of the socialist state are determined by the policies of the Marxist-Leninist party."

It is clear that we are discussing Soviet socialism and the system that was employed to further socialist development. The book *Political Economy: Socialism*, under the General Editorship of G.A. Kozlov, Progress Publishers, Moscow, 1977 has this to say on the justification of the economic role of the socialist state:

"The whole variety of tasks fulfilled by the socialist state can be reduced to two groups. The first is connected to administration...The second group is associated with planned organization of production, distribution, exchange and consumption of material wealth in socialist society. The activity of the socialist state in performing the first tasks belongs wholly to the sphere of relations in the superstructure, while performance of the second group, on the contrary, belongs to the realms of economic relations."

There is a certain interplay, of course, between the basis and superstructure., Lenin said, *'Politics is the concentrated expression of economics."* Politics is determined by economics, but in turn has an active influence on economics.

"At all stages of the development of the socialist system the *fundamentally new economic role of the socialist state* is expressed in its direction of the planned organization of production, distribution and exchange *and is wholly determined by socialist production relations, i.e. by the economic basis,* in the creation of which it is most actively involved.

For the first time in humanity the socialist state has become the state of the working people...The guiding and directing force of the socialist state is the Marxist-Leninist Party." (Passim, p.115)

As to the economic functions of the socialist state:

"The economic role of the socialist state is most diverse. Basing itself on economic laws and applying them consciously in its activities, the state organizes socialist production, plans the socialist economy and manages its operations; it also employs commodity-money relations in order to strengthen planned direction of the economy and develop the initiative of enterprises on the principle of profit-and-loss accounting. The state fixes the volume and structure of social production, investments and commodity circulation, decides the rates of growth of branches of the economy, organizes more and more rational distribution of the productive forces throughout the country and deals with the problems of developing all types of transport. It draws up and implements measures to promote scientific and technological progress, raise the efficiency of social production and labour productivity and to reduce costs of production and circulation. Through its proxies, the state manages the operation of public enterprises in all the spheres of the economy...organizes the work of millions of people and employs the country's labour resources in a planned way.

The socialist state organizes the distribution and use of the aggregate social product and national income. To further the growth of production and consumption it pursues a unified policy in relation to wages, institutes a system and procedure of payment for work in accordance with the socialist principle of distribution according to work and controls its implementation. The state determines the general level of prices and fixes prices for the most important types of product, organizes home and foreign trade and the working of the system of credit and finance, sees to the fulfillment of the budget, regulates the currency and encourages raising of the purchasing power of money. The state manages housing, public utilities and communal services and the health and social security services.

The socialist state maintains the economic, political and cultural ties between town and country, directs the development of agriculture, organizes the procurement of farm produce, guides the activities of co-operative and collective farm enterprises.

Public education is also within the competence of the socialist state... ...

The socialist state directs the economy on the basis of democratic centralism..." (Passim)

I have given these extensive quotes so as to make clear to the reader that these were the theoretical justification of the system of socialism that operated in the Soviet Union. These quotes show that from social ownership which is represented in the form of state ownership of the means of production developed a new role for the Socialist State within the Soviet Union's economy. The State became the dominant factor in the development of socialism in the Soviet Union. In fact, Kozlov has this to say on the role of the State in general:

"The socialist state is an instrument of strengthening and developing socialism and building communist society."

The theoreticians of Soviet 'Marxism-Leninism' extol the fact that the State plays a dominant role as an instrument in the development of socialism. Given the base-superstructure relation that forms the nub of Scientific Socialism, we see very clearly that the Socialist State is attributed with economic and social functions and apparatuses as part of socialist development, as having an *"active influence on economics"*. It is clear that the superstructure which arises out of the economic basis is going to react back on the basis but this is different from the socialist superstructure becoming the determining force of socialism led by the 'Marxist-Leninist Party'. The *essence* of the State changed under Soviet Socialism. It grew and developed not only coercive functions but also non-coercive functions in order to express state ownership of the means of production in the Soviet Union. The State was, thus, regarded as an instrument in the building of socialism and the transition to communism. The State became the fulcrum of economic development and acted as the basis, given the base-superstructure relationship. The State engaged in economic functions, the State acted as an economic agent. This was the *new approach* concerning the State in the epoch of 'World Socialism' dominated by the Soviet Union.

The State, under socialist conditions, according to Kozlov, was 'strengthened' with these economic and social functions in order to develop socialism and the transition to communism. Sheptulin argues, as 'Marxist-Leninist' philosophical justification, for this position thus;

"Socialist ownership of the means of production makes the socialist superstructure through the socialist state, the main distributor of the means of production and the nation-wide manager of the production processes. This means that, apart from its political functions, the socialist superstructure performs administrative and economic functions as well." (A. Sheptulin, "Marxist-Leninist Philosophy", Progress Publishers, 1978, p. 358.)

The system that the Soviet Union was based on was the *'State monopoly'* system. This was due to 'state ownership' being the dominant form of ownership of the means of production. State ownership led to the 'State monopoly' (Lenin's concept) system.

I look at this development in relation to the base-superstructure relationship of society. Given that the 'base' consists of the mode of production, there arises the relationship between *productive forces* and *relations of production*. In relation to the 'State-monopoly' system, it determines the relations of production as 'state relations'. 'State relations' act as economic relations of production. This is the logical position reached from the views of these theoreticians of Soviet 'Marxism-Leninism'. The theoretical significance of such a position is that the base and the superstructure, in the first place, become conflated, and secondly, the State dominates this development.

The 'State-monopoly' system sites the State as the determining lever, in the working people interests, in the development of socialism.

Roots of the State-monopoly system

These theoreticians of Soviet 'Marxism-Leninism' argued that the socialist State had to be developed, in their word 'strengthened', so that socialist development can take place. This 'strengthening' of the State has its roots in the history of the Soviet Union. This is what Stalin has to say on the matter:

"We are in favour of the State dying out, and at the same time we stand for the strengthening of the dictatorship of the proletariat, which represents the most powerful and mighty authority of all forms of State which have existed to the present day." (Stalin, 'Leninism', Vol.2, Political Report to Sixteenth Congress, p.402, Modern Books Limited, 1933.)

Stalin uses the word 'strengthening' in relation to the State. The Soviet theoreticians, cited above, also use the word 'strengthening'. This is their commonality. The understanding that we can reach from both uses of the word 'strengthening' is that there was developing a 'State-monopoly' system of socialism. The Soviet 'Marxist-Leninists' only developed what Stalin discussed in the 1930s.

The roots of this approach are to be found in the period of War Communism. This is what Lenin says on the matter:

"Surplus appropriation implied confiscation of all surpluses and establishment of a compulsory state monopoly...Theoretically speaking, state monopoly is not necessarily the best system from the standpoint of the interests of socialism." (Lenin, Selected Works, Vol.3, p.517, Progress Publishers, Moscow, 1977).

It should be aware to the reader that Lenin was aware of the state monopoly system. It was practiced during the period of War Communism. This was changed, on the authority of Lenin, to the Tax-in-Kind and the New Economic Policy. The reason for this change by Lenin was that the state monopoly system was not in the interests of socialism. Stalin reintroduced a new form of the state monopoly system under different conditions. This was through the Five and Ten-Year Plans. Centralized planning involved a new role for the State. The State was 'strengthened' with economic functions and also social and cultural functions. This had its roots in the aftermath of the October Revolution, the period of War Communism.

Implications

The system of socialism that prevailed in the Soviet Union after Lenin's death and especially in the second half of the twentieth century, the period of 'developed socialism', was the 'State-monopoly' system. This is the conclusion that has to be reached from the material available.

Soviet 'Marxism-Leninism', from Stalin onwards to its demise in the early 1990s, developed the position and raised it to the level of a scientific principle that the socialist State had to be 'strengthened'. This meant, in particular, of attributing the State with an economic role. This 'strengthening' of the State led it to become the dominant force in the building of socialism and in the period of 'developed socialism' especially in relation to the 'base'. The State was regarded as the determining force, as compared to the economy and civil society, in the building of socialism and the transition to communism. The socialist state as the dominant force in the building of socialism is led by the 'Marxist-Leninist Party'. It is the socialist state and the 'Marxist-Leninist Party' that determine the building of socialism. This position negates the fact that the workers are social owners of the means of production, are expressions of socialist relations of production and the task of the working class is to build socialism. This is the distortion of Scientific Socialist principles that 'Marxism-Leninism' engaged in.

This has implications for the 'base-superstructure' relationship of society as posited by Scientific Socialism. The 'strengthening' of the State leads it to act as an economic agent, and at times as the economy itself. There arises the category of the 'State economy'. The socialist State is not only conflated with the base but also begins to dominate it. This is a distortion of the principles of Scientific Socialism by Soviet 'Marxism-Leninism'.

Social ownership of the means of production should be reflected in the relations of production at the level of the base, the economy. It should not be reflected in the socialist State as happened in the Soviet Union through 'state ownership' because of the 'strengthening' of the State. The late Joe Slovo, former leader of the South African Communist Party, was quite correct to point out that there was an absence of socialist relations of production within Soviet Socialism in his pamphlet *Has Socialism Failed?* This absence of socialist relations of production was compensated by the 'State-monopoly' system with 'State relations'. This was another distortion of the principles of Scientific Socialism by Soviet Marxism-Leninism.

Lenin argued that the 'State-monopoly' system was not in the interests of Socialism. The 'strengthening' of the State led to the development of the 'State monopoly' system as the system of socialism in the USSR. Soviet 'Marxism-Leninism', from Stalin onwards, was guilty of developing a system that was not in the interests of the working people, not in the interests of socialism. This is another distortion of the principles of socialist development.

Conclusion

These are just some of the distortions that Soviet 'Marxism-Leninism' engaged whilst they were building socialism. They relied too much on the 'enthusiasm of the masses' and did not build a scientific socialist economy based on a scientific understanding of the 'base-superstructure' relationship within Socialism. Soviet Marxism-Leninism, from Stalin became enamored with the socialist State and saw it as means of solving economic problems in the building of socialism in the USSR. Through the 'state monopoly system', the Socialist State became omnipresent, omnipotent in determining the life of the working class in the Soviet Union. The consequence was the implosion of Soviet Socialism and the breakup of the USSR in 1991.

It is from the history of Scientific Socialism that I present my understanding of the 'Socialist Alternative'.

Marx in his discussion on the matter referred to co-operative societies as the basis of socialism arising out of the main contradiction of capitalism. Marx discussed, briefly, proletarian dictatorship in the era of socialism, in the era of co-operative societies. He laid down the basic theoretical rudiments of the system of socialism in the *Critique of the Gotha Programme*.

Marx argues that socialism is 'co-operative society based on common ownership of the means of production'. For Marx socialism is 'common ownership' of the means of production and the resulting economy is based on the co-operative system.

It was Lenin, who as leader of the socialist revolution in Soviet Russia, who came to definite conclusions concerning the system of socialism in Soviet Russia. It is clear that for Lenin to come to definite conclusions concerning the system of socialism for Soviet Russia there must have been a debate on the matter during that period. The question that must have been raised is: What is the system of socialism for Soviet Russia?

Lenin, in his article 'On Co-operation' in 1923, (Selected Works, Vol.3, Progress Publishers, Moscow, 1977) states:

"And given social ownership of the means of production, given the class victory of the proletariat over the bourgeoisie, the system of civilized co-operators is the system of socialism." (p.701)

Lenin substantiates this position thus:

"Indeed, since political power is in the hands of the working class, since this political power owns all the means of production, the only task, indeed, that remains for us is to organize the population in co-operative societies." (ibid, p.698)

Lenin gives an economic reason for arguing the position that the system of *"civilized co-operators is the system of socialism"*. This is what he says:

"All we actually need under NEP is to organize the population of Russia in co-operative societies on a sufficiently large scale, for we have now found that degree of combination of private interest, of private commercial interest, with state supervision and control of this interest, that degree of its subordination to the common interest..." (Pp.698-699)

Lenin points out that there should be material incentives for co-operatives such as a 'favourable bank rate'. The role of the socialist State is to take on a supervisory role. The State is not viewed as the dominant economic agent as Soviet 'Marxism-Leninism' treated the State.

For Lenin, the socialist economy, the mode of production or base, took the form of the co-operative system and the relations of production took the form of 'civilized co-operators'. This was the socialist base that Lenin envisaged for Soviet Russia. Socialist relations of production, which reflected social ownership of the means of production, had its representation in 'civilized co-operators'. The working class as 'civilized co-operators' is the builder of socialism. Lenin had resolved the base-superstructure relation given the conditions of Soviet Russia.

As regards the role of the superstructure through the socialist state, Lenin saw its role as being one of 'supervision and control'. Lenin did not call for the State to take on an economic role. This was Lenin's means of solving socialist development in Soviet Russia given the 'base-superstructure' relationship.

Lenin, through positing this system of 'civilized co-operators', correctly shows the relationship between proletarian dictatorship, that is to say, the State, and the socialist economy based on the co-operative mode of production. Lenin has this to say on 'proletarian dictatorship':

"But the essence of proletarian dictatorship is not in force alone, or even mainly in force. Its chief feature is the organization and discipline of the advanced contingent of the working people, of their vanguard; of their sole leader, the proletariat, whose object is to build socialism, abolish the division of society into classes, make all members of society working people, and remove the basis for all exploitation of man by man..." (Greetings to the Hungarian Workers, Selected Works, Vol.3, p.161. Progress Publishers, Moscow, 1977)

For Lenin, the system of civilized co-operators as the system of socialism was the basis for proletarian dictatorship. This was Lenin's vision of socialism in Soviet Russia.

Lenin argued that to develop the system of civilized co-operators as the system of socialism would take an historical epoch. At best, it could be achieved in one or two decades.

The important conclusion to be reached is that Marx came to the theoretical understanding that socialism would be based on 'co-operation' whereas Lenin comes to the same conclusion through social practice, through conducting the socialist revolution in Russia. The co-operative system as the system of socialism has its justification both theoretically and in practice within Scientific Socialism.

The situation changed with the development of Soviet 'Marxism-Leninism', from Stalin onwards. The emphasis was placed on the State as the determining role in the building of socialism in the USSR. This can be seen in the status accorded to the economic role of the State. The 'system of civilized co-operators' as expression of social ownership of the means of production, as expression of socialist relations of production did not become the dominant form. 'State relations' replaced it because of 'state ownership' of the means of production. Lenin's plan of socialism was not fully carried out by Stalin and the CPSU. This is the reason why there is an absence of socialist relations of production during the existence of the Soviet Union from Stalin onwards.

Socialism is on the political agenda. Capitalism at the stage of Globalization cannot solve the economic problems of working people, the social issues such as Poverty. It cannot solve the environmental crisis that is looming due to the capitalist drive for profits. It is now a question of understanding what the system of socialism is. This question is a vexatious question. The working people of the world have the history of Soviet socialism to learn from.

The main lesson is that the state monopoly system is not the system of socialism. The reason being is that it did not stand the test of time and failed to solve the very important question of socialist relations of production. Soviet Socialism, through its representation, Soviet 'Marxism-Leninism', developed the State as a means of building socialism in the Soviet Union. This is the reason why the cooperative basis did not become the dominant form of social ownership in the USSR.

Analysis

Lenin advocated the 'system of civilized co-operators' as the system of socialism for Soviet Russia. The 'system of civilized co-operators' is the mode of production of socialism as argued by Lenin. This did not develop in the subsequent history of the USSR. Rather, the 'State monopoly' system became the system of socialism in the USSR. It led to distortions in the mode of production and in production relations. Socialism has to find the appropriate relations of production, the appropriate mode of production in order to prove itself a higher economic form compared to capitalism. The distortion that the Soviet Union underwent with the implementation of the 'State monopoly' system meant that socialism could not prove itself, objectively, the higher form of social development as compared to capitalism. The 'state monopoly' system of Soviet socialism was always lagging behind capitalist development. The 'state monopoly' system in the Soviet Union could not satisfy the material wants and needs of its population, the working class.

Its 'stagnation' and its failure manifested itself in the 1980s in the Communist Party of the Soviet Union (CPSU) in the division between the Reformers and the Conservatives. I see it as the division between the 'Marxist-Leninists' and the 'Leninists'. The 'Marxist-Leninist's were for the state monopoly system as the system of socialism whereas in contrast the 'Leninists' were for the system of 'civilized co-operators' as the system of socialism. This division at the political level, within the CPSU, led to the demise of Soviet socialism.

Socialism has to show the dynamic balance between 'base' and 'superstructure'. The dictatorship of the proletariat cannot be expressed through the 'state monopoly' system as this breaks that delicate dynamic balance between base and superstructure. The 'essence of the dictatorship of the proletariat' does not lie in the 'strengthening' of the Socialist State. The social formation which is based on the 'state monopoly' system becomes too 'top heavy'. It leads to the development of a socialist bureaucracy which through the socialist State becomes the dominant factor in socialist society. It is the 'Marxist-Leninist' party that dominates the socialist bureaucracy. The Soviet Union suffered from this malaise in the stage of what Soviet 'Marxism-Leninism' called 'developed socialism'.

Socialism has to have appropriate relations of production. The development of the 'state monopoly' system led to an absence of socialist relations of production in the Soviet system. Lenin discovered the appropriate form, that of 'civilized co-operators', but its development was halted by the implementation of the 'state monopoly' system by Soviet 'Marxism-Leninism', from Stalin onwards. This distortion also contributed to the demise of Soviet Socialism.

I would like to give this quote from Marx's *Critique of the Gotha Programme*. This is what

Marx says:

"Freedom consists in converting the state from an organ superimposed upon society into one completely subordinate to it..."

The implementation of the 'state monopoly' system in the Soviet Union led to the State being an organ superimposed on socialist society. The State became the dominant force in socialist society. Civil Society and economic relations played a subordinate role to the State. This is the lesson to be learnt from adopting the 'state monopoly' system as the system of socialism. It contributed to the demise of Soviet socialism. The future of socialist development lies with developing a 'co-operative' base and the State being subordinate to the base and civil society.

I gave a quote from Marx concerning his attitude to the proletarian revolutions of the nineteenth century in the beginning of the essay. The twentieth century saw the world's first socialist revolution. It spawned other socialist revolutions. The twentieth century also saw the passing away of socialist revolutions. There was the implosion of 'World Socialism'. This is at the early stage of socialist development that is being observed by the world. The Communists should be self-critical in these early attempts at building socialism as society moves from the pre-historical stage to the historical stage of development. I say this because as a former 'Marxist-Leninist' educator in Britain, I see modern 'Marxism-Leninism' as dogmatic and obscurantist in approach. This is clearly seen when it adopts the 'state monopoly' system as the system of socialism by advocating 'state ownership' or 'public ownership' of the means of production. This approach, as Lenin pointed out, is not in the 'interest of socialism'.

It fails to take into account the history of the working class. Lenin, when he called for the system of 'civilized co-operators' as the system of socialism, took into account the history of the working class co-operative movement. This is the difference between the 'Marxist-Leninist' position and the position of Lenin in the building of socialism in Soviet Russia.

This lesson has not been studied scientifically within Communist circles. The 'Marxist-Leninists' who dominate the International Communist Movement still attribute a developmental role, of an economic nature, for the State which is not its function. Lenin pointed to the 'essence' of proletarian dictatorship as being concerned with a non-coercive role in furthering the interests of the working class. He did not argue that the essence of proletarian dictatorship consisted in the 'strengthening' of the State.

Scientific Socialism has to discuss these problems critically in the twenty first century if it is to show itself as serious about social development, serious about the transition to socialism. The lessons of Soviet Socialism have to be studied scientifically and mistakes rectified in preparing a programme for the transition to socialism. 'Marxism-Leninism' has shown itself as distorting the basic principles of Scientific Socialism when it adopted the 'State-monopoly system' as the system of socialism based on 'state ownership' or 'public ownership. 'Marxism-Leninism' stands on the pedestal of dogmatism which leads it to developing an obscurantist approach thus distorting the principles of Scientific Socialism.

The question that is raised in the twenty first century is: "What is the system of Socialism?" China is developing its own New Economic Policy which is concerned with using capitalism to further develop the productive forces for examples, Shanghai and Hong Kong. It's economy, however, is based on the State monopoly system. China's future development is faced with this question. It is the largest communist country and the second largest economy in the world. If it is not to regress to capitalism as Russia has done, then it has to solve the problems that the above question poses. The few countries that have embarked on the socialist path of development have to develop the co-operative system as the system of socialism in order that socialism proves itself as the higher form of social production compared to capitalism.

The implosion of 'World Socialism' and the Soviet Union has to lead to a reassessment of the present understanding of the question 'What is socialism?'
It is interesting to understand the position of the 'Marxist-Leninist' Communist Party of Britain (CPB) in the *British Road to Socialism* as expressed by one of its senior party members, Mary Davis, on its website (2012). She states:

"Socialist public ownership would end monopoly capitalist control of the economy and in doing so would put an end to the exploitation of the working class because surplus labour would no longer be performed for capitalist profit."

Mary Davis sees the solution to monopoly capital 'control' and 'exploitation of the working class' in 'socialist public ownership'. 'Socialist public ownership' can only develop state ownership of the means of production through socialist nationalization of the means of production. 'Socialist public ownership' leads to the 'State' becoming engaged in economic activity. 'Socialist public ownership' leads to the 'strengthening' of the 'State'. 'Socialist public ownership' means that that the 'State' becomes the determining force in the building of socialism not the working class. 'Socialist public ownership' is the negation of socialist relations of production. 'Socialist public ownership' appears, according to Mary Davis reasoning, to be the system of socialism once exploitation of the working class has ended. This position of Mary Davis is in contradiction to Lenin's position that *"the system of civilized co-operators is the system of socialism"*. This is how the 'Marxist-Leninist' Mary Davis distorts the principles of Scientific Socialism.

'Marxism-Leninism' sees the State as an economic agent in an absolute sense. The State, which is 'relatively autonomous' from the 'base', becomes the dominant force in the building of socialism. It is the 'civilized co-operators' who build socialism not the State and the Communist Party. In this sense, 'socialist public ownership' which involves state ownership of the means of production, makes the 'state' into a form that is superimposed on working people not subordinate to it. The 'Marxist-Leninist' Mary Davis and the Communist Party of Britain do not understand the writings of Marx and Lenin on socialism and its system. Moreover, both Mary Davis and the CPB have failed to analyze scientifically the Soviet system.

It is important to understand 'Marxism-Leninism' avowal of 'state ownership' or 'public ownership' of the means of production. 'Marxism-Leninism' argues that social or 'common' ownership of the means of production is expressed in 'state ownership' or 'public ownership' of the means of production. As the most advanced form of social ownership, 'state ownership' allows the socialist State to be the determining element in the socialist economy. 'State ownership' arises through socialist nationalization of the means of production. This is what the 'Marxist-Leninist' Mary Davis means by 'socialist public ownership' which can only arise through socialist nationalization of the means of production. For 'Marxism-Leninism', socialist nationalization of the means of production plays an important economic role because it expresses 'state ownership' or 'socialist public ownership' and the dominant role of the socialist State.

The first point to note is that 'state ownership' is not advocated by the founders of Scientific Socialism, Marx and Engels, and by Lenin.

The second point to note is that 'state ownership' distorts the base-superstructure relationship. At the beginning of this Essay I gave quotes from Soviet 'Marxist-Leninists' concerning property forms in the Soviet Union which they stated were basically two: state property based on state ownership and co-operative property forms. These two forms of property relations lead to two different systems: the 'system of civilized co-operators' or the co-operative system and the 'state monopoly' system. The co-operative property form has its roots in 'common ownership' whereas 'state ownership' involves turning 'common ownership' into 'state ownership'. The experiences of the Soviet Union from Stalin onwards show that they cannot co-exist with each other because they contradict each other. This contradiction has to be resolved. One system has to be the determining element in the 'building of socialism'. This is why Stalin *neglected* (for want of a better word) Lenin's position of organizing the working people and the working class of Soviet Russia in co-operatives, the 'system of civilized co-operators' and chose 'state ownership' leading to 'state monopoly' as the dominant system. It took nearly seventy years, from the 1930s to the early 1990s, of Soviet experience to show the world that the 'state monopoly' system based on 'state ownership' is not the system of socialism.

The socialist State cannot express ownership of the means of production through 'state ownership' because that gives it a dominant economic role that leads to distortions in the relations of production which leads to distortions in the base-superstructure relationship. This was the case in both the Soviet Union and 'World Socialism' which adopted the 'Marxist-Leninist' model of the system of socialism, the 'state monopoly' system. Social ownership of the means of production cannot be expressed through the socialist State, through 'state ownership' but only in relations of production, at the level of the base. That is why Lenin's scientific concept of 'civilized co-operators' is very important for Scientific Socialism because it sites social ownership of the means of production in socialist relations of production through the form of 'civilized co-operators' at the level of the 'base'. The socialist working class ownership of the means of production cannot be expressed through the socialist State because it's, the socialist working class, *"object is to build socialism"* (Lenin) and not that of 'strengthening' the State. The task of the socialist State is to ensure the conditions of working class ownership of the means of production and the building of socialism, the system of 'civilized co-operators' which is the mode of production, prevails. For Lenin, at the level of the socialist base there existed the relation between socialist forces of production and socialist relations of production, that of 'civilized co-operators', the owners of the means of production. On this arose a socialist superstructure, including the socialist State, which has to be subordinate to the interests of the working class. This was Lenin's system of socialism

The third point to note is that socialist nationalization of the means of production which leads to 'state ownership' or 'public ownership' and which gives the Socialist State the dominant role in the economy does not accord with the principles of Scientific Socialism. This is what the CPB has stated on its website:

"Only public ownership of the economy's major sectors and enterprises – the economic essence of socialism – can put an end to monopoly power and fundamentally change the

basis on which economic decisions are taken." (Website, April 2012)

It is clear that the 'Marxist-Leninist' CPB sees 'public ownership' as the 'economic essence of socialism'. Mary Davis uses the notion 'socialist public ownership. This is where the 'Marxist-Leninist' Mary Davis goes wrong. She sees 'socialist public ownership' as the system of socialism that ends capitalist exploitation of the working class. It must be pointed out to her that socialism ends capitalist exploitation of the working class and that the system of socialism, as pointed out by Lenin, is the system of 'civilized co-operators'. She blinds herself to Scientific Socialism by advocating 'socialist public ownership'. For the CPB, the 'economic essence of socialism' is in 'public ownership' or 'state ownership'. Where did the CPB get its position that 'public ownership' is the 'essence of socialism'? It is certainly not from the founders of Scientific Socialism, Marx and Engels or from Lenin. Marx argued that the 'essence' of socialism is 'co-operative society based on common ownership of the means of production'. 'Marxism-Leninism' suffers from the disease of blindness to the writings on socialism by Marx, Engels and Lenin.

Property ownership and property relations cannot be based in the socialist State, on the socialist superstructure through 'state ownership'. Property ownership and property relations are economic categories which have to be sited at the level of the base not in the superstructure as 'Marxism-Leninism' does with 'state ownership'. The socialist superstructure, including the socialist State, will reflect and represent property ownership and property relations at the level of the base which is working class ownership of the means of production expressed in socialist relations of production in the form of 'civilized co-operators'. 'State ownership' is not identical with working class ownership of the means of production. Lenin identified working class ownership of the means of production through the economic concept, that of 'civilized co-operators'. Lenin sites socialist property ownership at the level of the base and its expression through socialist relations of production, that of 'civilized co-operators'. This is the difference between Lenin's position and 'Marxism-Leninism'.

For 'Marxism-Leninism' co-operative property forms are secondary to 'state ownership'. The latter is the most advanced form as compared to the former. There is an inversion of property ownership by 'Marxism-Leninism'. 'State ownership' has become the dominant expression of social ownership and 'co-operative' ownership, the real economic form of property ownership within socialism, becomes secondary or subordinate to 'state ownership'. In addition, the notion of 'public ownership' or 'state ownership', or 'socialist public ownership' being the 'essence of socialism' is an 'inversion' of the' base- superstructure' relations. An 'inversion' in which state property forms through 'state ownership' or 'socialist public ownership' leading to 'state monopoly' results in the domination of the 'superstructure' over the 'base'.

For Lenin, 'civilized co-operators' expressed, scientifically, socialist relations of production which made co-operative property ownership the dominant form. This is the difference in the positions of Lenin and 'Marxism-Leninism'. It is important to be critical of the 'Marxist-Leninist' notion that the most advanced form of social ownership of the means of production is 'state ownership' or 'public ownership'. It leads to the alienation of the working class from direct ownership of the means of production as happened in the USSR. It leads to the negation of the base and its role in the building of socialism. It is the working class that builds socialism as pointed out by Lenin not the socialist State.

What 'Marxism-Leninism' has done is to identify social ownership with 'state ownership' or 'public ownership'. 'Social ownership' and 'state ownership' are not identical. The task of the superstructure and the state is to reflect and represent the forms of social ownership at the level of the base. It is not to assume relations at the level of the base through 'state ownership'.

The importance of 'state ownership' for 'Marxism-Leninism' has to be understood. It gave the socialist state led by the 'Marxist-Leninist' party 'control of social production'. The socialist state was responsible for the planned development of the economy. Central planning was determined by the socialist state and the 'Marxist-Leninist' party. Soviet 'Marxism-Leninism' developed a law which was called the *"The Law of Planned Proportionate Development of Social Production"*. This is what Ryndina *et al* (whom I have mentioned earlier) state:

"Under socialism there is the domination of social ownership of the means of production, national state ownership playing the leading and determining role. The latter makes the national economy into a single production organism, one giant enterprise. Production is socialized on the scale of the entire national economy. ...Planned development becomes the universal form of development of social production. It embraces production proper, distribution, exchange and the consumption of material goods and services. Being characteristic of socialist production relations the planned proportionate development of social production becomes an economic law of socialism...Planned regulation is conducted by the socialist state..." (Passim, pp237-239)

These Soviet 'Marxist-Leninist' theoreticians argued that from 'national state ownership' there arises a 'national economy' which is 'one giant enterprise' where production is socialized leading to planning becoming *"the universal form of development of social production"*. This leads to the *"planned proportionate development of social production"* becoming an 'economic law' because it is characteristic of 'socialist production relations'. Planning is conducted by the socialist state. This is how Soviet 'Marxism-Leninism' constructed 'laws' of socialism.

Central planning must be sited at the level of the base not the superstructure, the socialist State. It must be sited at the level of the base through a commission that is democratically accountable to the 'civilized co-operators'. The role of the state is, as Lenin pointed out, 'supervision and control' not being the dominant force in central planning as determined by the so-called law of *"Planned proportionate development of social production"*.

'Marxism-Leninism' propagates 'state ownership', 'socialist public ownership' but it is 'silent' on the critical issue of what 'form' socialist relations of production will take. The absence of socialist relations of production in the Soviet Union, as pointed out by the late Joe Slovo, also contributed to the alienation of the working class from the building of socialism. This was the reason why Soviet 'Marxism-Leninism' could not scientifically explain socialist relations of production. Kozlov, when he discusses production relations and economic interests (p.74) talks about "The Leading Role of the National Interest" and other things but does not define socialist relations of production as Lenin did with 'civilized co-operators'. This is where 'Marxism-Leninism' differs from the writings of Lenin on socialism. This is where 'Marxism-Leninism' differs from the writings of Marx on the socialist base-superstructure relationship.

The base-superstructure relationship is very important for Scientific Socialism as developed by Marx because it shows how society functions. The base- superstructure relationship acts as tools of analysis for social formations including the socialist social formation. It should be clear that Lenin with his concept of 'civilized co-operators' adheres to Marx's understanding of relations of production under conditions of socialist development in Soviet Russia.

The base-superstructure relationship, as Lenin realized, is very important in determining the system of socialism. With his concept of 'civilized co-operators', Lenin develops the determining role of the base and how it affects the socialist superstructure including the socialist state. This is why he argued that the system of socialism is 'the system of civilized co-operators'. The co-operative system at the level of the base will have socialist relations of production in the form of 'civilized co-operators' that will determine the role of the socialist superstructure, including the socialist State. The socialist State has to be subordinate to the base where the interests of working people in general and the working class in particular lie.

I have compared and contrasted the positions of Lenin and 'Marxism-Leninism' so as to understand the question "What is the system of socialism?" The failures of the 'State monopoly system' have to be analyzed and assessed scientifically so that revolutionary theory can be raised to a higher level. More importantly, through the domination of 'Marxism-Leninism' in the International Communist Movement, Scientific Socialism is standing on its head. This is what 'Marxism-Leninism' has done to Scientific Socialism.

'Marxism-Leninism' has distorted the base-superstructure relation under socialist conditions by giving the socialist state the dominant role in the national economy through 'state ownership' or 'socialist public ownership'. 'State ownership' negates socialist relations of production and the socialist state cannot be the driving force of the socialist base or economy. The 'state monopoly system' that arises out of 'state ownership' did not meet the material needs and wants of the working class in the Soviet Union. This was the basic economic failure of the 'state monopoly system' in the USSR.

One of the shoots of socialism arising out of the womb of capitalism is the Co-operative Movement. Co-operative property forms are developing within capitalism. Monopoly capital in Britain cannot destroy the Co-operative Movement and its property forms. In fact, one of its bourgeois politicians, David Cameron, the British Prime Minister, talks about linking the Co-operative Movement to capitalism more fully as it is doing well in austerity-hit Britain. Will the Co-operative Movement develop into a future system of socialism in Britain? There can be no returning to the 'state monopoly system' or any variant, that is to say, 'socialist public ownership' as advocated by the 'Marxist-Leninist', Mary Davis. 'Marxism-Leninism' has not learnt the lessons of 'developed socialism' in the Soviet Union. It still advocates 'state ownership' or 'socialist public ownership'. Mary Davis of the Communist Party of Britain is the classic example. That is why I have mentioned her position on the system of socialism.

The treatment of co-operative property forms as secondary to 'state ownership', as less 'advanced', by 'Marxism-Leninism' does a disservice to the working class who are responsible for the building of 'co-operative society' and to Lenin's position. It negates the role of the working class in the building of the 'co-operative system' of socialism. Modern 'Marxism-Leninism' subordinates co-operative property forms to 'public' or 'state ownership' since the time of Stalin. 'Public' or 'state ownership' of the means of production which leads to the 'state monopoly' system has its 'basis' in 'Stalinism' not Scientific Socialism.

The future of socialism lies in the co-operative movements developing world-wide. It does not lie in 'state ownership' of the means of production and the dominating role of the socialist State in the functioning of socialist economy or base. 'Marxism-Leninism' is incorrect in its position on the system of socialism.

I conclude by looking at the position of the 'Marxist-Leninist' Communist Party of Britain (CPB) on the system of socialism in the USSR or Soviet Union. This is what they state in their programme, *The British Road to Socialism*:

"...In particular, a bureaucratic-command system of economic and political rule became entrenched. The Communist Party of the Soviet Union and trade unions became integrated into the apparatus of the state, eroding working class and popular democracy. Marxism-Leninism was used dogmatically to justify the status quo, rather than make objective assessments of it."

In general, the CPB is critical of the system of the Soviet Union. They, however, call the system of socialism in the Soviet Union a 'bureaucratic-command system'. The CPB fails to understand that the system of socialism in the Soviet Union was the 'state monopoly system' not a 'bureaucratic-command system'. The CPB is blind to the scientific concept of Lenin, that is, 'state monopoly' and thus its analysis is unscientific and smacks of a Trotskyite analysis. This analysis fails to take into account materialist premises. The CPB does not begin its analysis from the base-superstructure relation of analyzing society as Marx stated. A 'bureaucratic-command system' looks too much at super-structural features and does not look at the relations that exist at the level of the base.

The CPB fails to understand that 'Marxism-Leninism' was developed to justify the 'state monopoly system' that existed in the Soviet Union. The CPB is correct to say that *"Marxism-Leninism was used dogmatically to justify the status quo..."* The 'status quo' was not 'a bureaucratic-command system' but the 'state monopoly system' led by the 'Marxist-Leninist' Communist Party of the Soviet Union.

Within 'Marxism-Leninism' there are different analyses of the system of the Soviet Union. In this case, the 'Marxist-Leninist' Communist Party of Britain is incorrect.

'Marxism-Leninism', in the second decade of the twenty first century, still holds fast to 'state ownership' or 'socialist public ownership' of the means of production. The South African Communist Party (SACP) and the Communist Party of Britain, for example, hold fast to 'state ownership' of the means of production. 'Marxism-Leninism' has not learnt the lessons of the failures of the 'state monopoly system' that existed in the Soviet Union based on 'state ownership' or 'public ownership'.

Scientific Socialism stands for the co-operative system as the system of socialism. Scientific Socialism does not state that the 'economic essence of socialism' is 'public ownership' or 'state ownership' as 'Marxism-Leninism' does. This is the major difference between 'Marxism-Leninism' and Scientific Socialism.

It is important to look at the position of the South African Communist Party (SACP) in its South African Road to Socialism (SARS) on its understanding of socialism which is on its Website. This is what the SACP argues:

"Socialism is a transitional social system between capitalism ...and a fully classless, communist society. A socialist society has a mixed economy, but one in which the socialized component of the economy is dominant and hegemonic. The socialized economy is that part

of the economy premised on meeting social needs and not private profits."

Let us look at the proposition that socialism is a 'transitional social system' between capitalism and communism. The first point to note is what Marx stated. Marx argued that socialism is the 'first phase' of communist society. Marx wrote briefly on socialism. However, he did not argue that socialism was a 'transitional social system' between capitalism and communist society.

The second point to note is that the SACP argues that *"socialist society has a mixed economy."* In the *Critique of the Gotha Programme* Marx argued that socialism or 'socialist society' is *"co-operative society based on common ownership of the means of production".* Marx did not argue that socialism has a 'mixed economy'. Lenin did not depict Soviet Russia has having a 'mixed economy' but stated that the co-operative system is the system of socialism.

The SACP position is abstract and over-generalized. The SACP begins with the proposition that socialism is a 'transitional system' between capitalism and communism and thus concludes with the assertion that the socialist society has a 'mixed economy'. This position contradicts Lenin's position that 'the system of civilized co-operators is the system of socialism'. The arguments of the 'Marxist-Leninist' SACP show how far it is from the position of Marx and Lenin. Lenin agreed with Marx when he argued that 'the system of civilized co-operators is the system of socialism'. The co-operative system, for these two great revolutionaries, is the system of socialism. This is how far the 'Marxist-Leninist' SACP has strayed from the principles of Scientific Socialism. This shows how the 'Marxist-Leninist' SACP is 'making-up' theory on socialism when it advocates 'state ownership' or 'public ownership' and the 'strengthening' of the 'State' in the second phase of the National Democratic Revolution which is to be socialist orientated.

'Marxism-Leninism' has not developed socialist society based on the co-operative system. 'Marxism-Leninism' has been engaged in developing socialism based on 'state ownership' or 'socialist public ownership' leading to the 'state monopoly' system. This is the difference between 'Marxism-Leninism' and Scientific Socialism.

The obsessive advocacy of 'public ownership' under socialism, of 'socialist public ownership' by 'Marxism-Leninism' blinds it to the fact that the 'state monopoly' system in the USSR and Eastern European countries in the second half of the twentieth century which embarked on the socialist path of development led to the 'alienation' of the working class from the means of production. I have used Marx's concept briefly but at this juncture I would like to discuss it.

Socialism, the 'first phase' of communism, which is 'co-operative society based on common ownership of the means of production' according to Marx, is engaged in overcoming the 'alienation' that the worker and the working class experience under capitalism. Socialism, based on the co-operative system, is concerned with the worker and the working class being at one with the means of production due to 'common ownership' expressed in 'co-operative property relations'.

In contrast, the 'state monopoly' system based on 'state' or 'public' ownership that prevailed in the second half of the twentieth century in the Soviet Union and the eastern European countries saw the expression of 'alienation' of the working class, of the worker, from the means of production, from the 'building of socialism'. It is intrinsic to the 'state monopoly' system that 'alienation' will develop because being based on 'state' or 'socialist public ownership' and socialist nationalization of the means of production the worker and the working class become 'estranged' from the means of production. On the other hand, the 'state' becomes 'strengthened' and led by the Communist Party, as happened in the Soviet Union and the Eastern European countries which adopted the Soviet 'model', becomes the dominating force and superimposes itself on the 'economy' and society. The 'building of socialism' (Lenin) becomes the function of the socialist State and the Communist Party and negates the role of the working class in the 'building of socialism'. This happened in the Soviet Union when there began the 'state monopoly' system based on 'state ownership' or 'public ownership' from Stalin onwards. In the early part of this essay I gave quotes from Soviet 'Marxist-Leninists' who justified the role of the State in the 'building of socialism' not only to show that they developed the 'state monopoly' system but also to show that by adopting such a system they failed to realize that it would lead to the 'alienation' of the working class from the 'building of socialism'. This contradiction between the State and the working class in the 'building of socialism' arises out of the adoption of the 'state monopoly' system based on the contradiction between 'state ownership' and co-operative property forms which ultimately led to the 'alienation' of the working class because of the emphasis on the State and the Communist Party as opposed to the working class. It was the late Joe Slovo of the SACP who made me aware of 'alienation' under socialism but his analysis is limited although he broke new ground in the discussion of socialism in his work *'Has Socialism Failed'*. I hope I have done him justice by explaining the root cause of 'alienation' in the Soviet Union and the eastern European countries.

Slovo is correct that there was an absence of socialist relations of production leading to the 'alienation' of the working class from the 'building of socialism'. The limitation of his analysis is that he fails to analyze the Soviet system. The Soviet system of 'state monopoly' based on 'state ownership' or 'public ownership' or even Mary Davis's notion of 'socialist public ownership' leads to an 'absence of socialist relations of production' which leads to the 'alienation' of the working class from the 'building of socialism'.

Lenin pointed the way. From his statement that 'the system of civilized co-operators is the system of socialism' there develops the co-operative mode of production which develops socialist relations of production in the form of 'civilized co-operators' which is engaged in the 'building of socialism'. The State becomes an 'enabler', 'facilitator' and 'provider' for the working class/ 'civilized co-operators' to fulfill its role of 'building socialism'. The task of the State is to engage in 'supervision' and control' in order that the working class fulfill its role of 'building socialism'. Given this 'condition of existence' there is the negation of 'alienation'. The co-operative mode of production or system negates the feature of 'alienation' that arises from the 'state monopoly system' based on 'state ownership' or 'public ownership'.

It is important to analyze the position of 'Marxism-Leninism' on the Soviet Union. For 'Marxism- Leninism', socialism existed in the Soviet Union. It saw it through the paradigms of 'existing socialism' or 'developed socialism' (these notions are too generalised). On this basis, the 'Marxist-Leninist' CPB invokes the notion of a 'bureaucratic-command system,' which they argue, developed in the USSR that led to the implosion of the Soviet Union and socialism. A 'bureaucratic-command system' cannot develop on the basis of 'state ownership' or 'public ownership'. The dominant property relations that existed in the Soviet Union, from Stalin to Gorbachev, were 'state ownership' or 'public ownership' which led to the 'state monopoly' system. The 'state monopoly system', based on the State, develops a socialist bureaucracy and a 'command' structure which reinforces the 'state monopoly system'. The 'state monopoly' system and its socialist bureaucracy were dominated by the Communist Party of the Soviet Union (CPSU). This was the case in the Soviet Union. It was the CPSU and the Socialist State that was responsible for 'state planning' of the 'economy' and society. It was this domination by the 'Marxist-Leninist' CPSU in the 'building of socialism' that resulted in the 'alienation' of the working class in the 'building of socialism'. The Party became the 'force of attraction' in the 'building of socialism' not the working class. The 'state monopoly' system dictated to the working class within 'developed socialism' in the USSR. The 'state monopoly' system was in this sense not an expression of the 'dictatorship of the proletariat' because of the 'alienation' of the working class. 'Socialist public ownership' or 'state ownership' or 'public ownership' as the dominant property relations is not an expression of the 'dictatorship of the proletariat'.

The only property relations that express scientifically the 'dictatorship of the proletariat are 'co-operative' property relations which engage the working class as 'civilized co-operators' in the 'building of socialism' and thus negating 'alienation' within socialist society. The working class through the form of socialist relations of production known as 'civilized co-operators' becomes the 'force of attraction' in the expression of the 'dictatorship of the proletariat.

It should be clear that there are differences between 'Marxism-Leninism' and Scientific Socialism. 'Marxism-Leninism' was the ideology that was developed in the Soviet Union to justify the 'State-Monopoly system'. 'Marxism-Leninism' has become a dogma that is stifling the working class from learning the lessons of the 'failures' of 'socialism' that developed in the twentieth century. 'Marxism-Leninism', especially those 'Marxist-Leninist' organizations like the Communist Party of Britain, when they state that 'public ownership' is the 'essence of socialism' does a disservice to the working class. The CPB has seriously failed to develop a scientific analysis of the Soviet system so as to show the way to the working class of Britain. The CPB, when it talks about 'socialist public ownership', has to conclude that relations of production take the form of 'public employees' or 'public workers' or 'state employees or workers'. I contrast 'public workers', which the CPB would probably develop, to Lenin's 'civilized co-operators' and it is clear that Lenin's concept is the correct expression for socialist relations of production. Furthermore, 'public workers' or 'state employees' which arise out of 'state' or 'public' ownership are not scientific expressions of socialist relations of production as Lenin's concept 'civilized co-operators' is. Moreover, 'public workers', as compared to Lenin's 'civilized co-operators', is an 'alienated' expression of the working class based on 'public ownership'. This is the fundamental difference between Lenin's position and 'Marxism-Leninism', between Scientific Socialism and 'Marxism-Leninism'.

Secondly, and this is very important, 'state ownership or 'public ownership' or even 'socialist public ownership' is not an expression of 'social ownership' or 'common ownership' (Marx) of the means of production. For Marx and Lenin, 'social' or 'common ownership' is expressed in 'Co-operation', in the co-operative mode of production, in 'co-operative society' (Marx), in 'civilized co-operators' (Lenin), not in 'state ownership' leading to 'state monopoly'. 'Social ownership' or 'common ownership' has to be expressed at the level of the 'base' not in the 'superstructure' through the State, through 'state ownership' as 'Marxism-Leninism' does. This is why Lenin's Scientific Socialist concept 'civilized co-operators' is very important. It sites 'working class ownership' or 'social ownership' or 'common ownership' at the level of the 'base' in the form of socialist relations of production in 'civilized co-operators'. The notion that 'social' or 'common ownership' is expressed in 'state ownership' is a false and misleading notion that 'Marxism-Leninism' has propagated since the time of Stalin. It is this 'baggage' of 'Stalinism' that 'Marxism-Leninism' propagates as socialism. This is very much the case with the Communist Party of Britain and the South African Communist Party.

'In the final analysis', 'Marxism-Leninism' argues for the 'strengthening' of the State within socialism based on 'public' or 'state' ownership. In relation to the CPB, their statement that 'public ownership' is the 'essence of socialism' leads to the 'strengthening' of the socialist State because 'public ownership' is expressed as 'state ownership' which leads to 'state monopoly'. The South African Communist Party calls for the 'strengthening' of the National Democratic State in the second, socialist orientated phase of the National Democratic Revolution in South Africa. From these two examples it is clear that 'Marxism-Leninism' follows Stalin in calling for the 'strengthening' of the State. The experience of the Soviet system of 'state monopoly' was that the socialist State was 'strengthened' so much that it negated the Scientific Socialist principle of the 'withering away of the State'.

Scientific Socialism takes a principled position on the State. Scientific Socialism, according to Marx, is concerned with the' withering away of the State' which means not 'strengthening' the State. Scientific Socialism states that for socialist 'freedom' to exist the State must be subordinated to society and not 'superimposed' on it.

With the advocacy of 'state monopoly' based on 'public' or 'state' ownership being the 'essence of socialism', by 'Marxism-Leninism', the State, which is responsible for socialist planning and directs the economy and led by the 'Marxist-Leninist' Party, becomes 'superimposed' on socialist society. This was the experience of the Soviet Union. The 'superimposition' of the State on Soviet society due to the 'state monopoly' system based on 'state' ownership and led by the 'Marxist-Leninist' Communist Party of the Soviet Union (CPSU) resulted in the 'alienation' of the working class from the 'building of socialism'.

The quote from Stalin, in the early part of this Essay, on the 'strengthening' and 'withering away' of the State and the 'dictatorship of the proletariat' led to the domination of the State, its 'superimposition', on Soviet society, based on 'state ownership' leading to 'state monopoly', shows that such an approach is not necessarily the best system from the standpoint of the interest of socialism as Lenin pointed out correctly. Moreover, Stalin by talking about 'strengthening' and 'withering away' of the State develops a contradiction between these two 'opposites' which resulted in the State being 'strengthened' and not 'wither away' which eventually led to the implosion of socialism in the Soviet Union. Stalin equates the 'dictatorship of the proletariat' with the 'State' and this is quite different from the quote by Lenin on the same subject which has been provided in the early part of this Essay (see 'Greetings to the Hungarian Workers') The experience of the role of the socialist State in the Soviet Union, as it was 'directed' by the 'Marxist-Leninist' CPSU, shows that it did not accord with the principles of Scientific Socialism.

The quotes from Soviet 'Marxist-Leninists', which was given at the beginning of this Essay, shows clearly the role of the State in the 'building of socialism'. There occurred a 'fetishism', similar to 'commodity fetishism' which Marx talked about, on the role of the State by Soviet 'Marxism-Leninism' to the cost of the working class in the 'building of socialism'.

The 'Marxist-Leninist' Communist Party of Britain (CPB) statement that 'public ownership…is the essence of socialism' similarly shows a 'fetish' for 'public ownership' of the means of production. This is more apparent with Mary Davis's notion 'socialist public ownership'. It is not only 'fetishism' but an 'obsession' as well by the CPB and its 'leading lights'. The CPB argues for 'public ownership' under capitalism and then goes on to state that the 'essence of socialism' is 'public ownership'. The only problem with the CPB position is that it becomes blind to the historical experience that 'public ownership' leads to 'state monopoly'.

This 'fetish' for 'public ownership', nay, 'socialist public ownership' not only leads to 'state monopoly' but results in 'state central planning' which is determined by the economic policies of the 'Marxist-Leninist' Communist Party. Soviet 'Marxist-Leninists', Ryndina and co, cited above, let the cat out of the bag by stating thus:

"The most important planning principle consists in its party spirit. In socialist society, planning has a truly partisan character. It embodies the economic policy of the Marxist-Leninist party. Every economic plan represents a particular stage in the implementation of the party's programme and is aimed at the building of socialism and communism." (p.245)

The 'building of socialism' is the task of the working class involving the expression of the 'dictatorship of the proletariat'. In the Soviet Union, with the 'state monopoly system', there developed not the 'dictatorship of the proletariat' but the 'dictatorship of the Party'. This is clearly seen in the development of 'state central planning' which expressed the economic policy of the 'Marxist-Leninist' Party. Similarly, the CPB statement that 'public ownership… is the essence of socialism' leads to its economic policy being the 'essence' of 'state central planning'. This view of the 'essence' of socialism based on 'socialist public ownership' or 'public ownership' is nothing more than 'Stalinism' in disguise. This 'view' does not have its roots in the principles of Scientific Socialism. This 'view' which is prevalent and dominates 'Communist ideology' in the present era is a travesty and distortion of the principles of Scientific Socialism on socialism as developed by Marx and Lenin. This 'view' as represented by 'Marxism-Leninism' has nothing to do with Scientific Socialism and is not in the interest of the working class let alone in the 'interests of socialism' (Lenin).

It is important to be clear on the meaning' of 'public ownership' or 'socialist public ownership'. In a sense, 'public ownership' or 'socialist public ownership' reflects social ownership. Within the capitalist mode of production, within capitalism in the twentieth century, 'public ownership' meant 'state ownership' of industries resulting in state enterprises controlled by the State as evidenced in the case of Britain in the post-War period (British Telecom, British Gas). In the Soviet Union, social ownership came to be viewed in terms of 'state ownership'. Social practice in the twentieth century showed that 'public ownership' is synonymous with 'state ownership'.

The Soviet 'model', the system of 'state monopoly', based on 'state ownership' or 'public ownership', that began in the 1930s and ended in the early 1990s showed clearly, through social practice, that it failed to meet the needs and wants of its population, the working class of the Soviet Union.

Scientific Socialism argues that 'public ownership' or 'socialist public ownership' which leads to the system of 'state monopoly' concerning the 'commanding heights of the economy' is not the system of socialism as 'Marxism-Leninism', in the representation of the

CPB, argues.

Scientific Socialism states that the co-operative system is the system of socialism, the mode of production for socialist society based on 'common ownership' or social ownership. In this context, there comes to the fore Marx's concept of 'co-operative labour'. It is clear that there needs to be a discussion on this concept and its importance for socialism. 'Co-operative labour' will produce a surplus, which will be used in the interests of the institutions of socialism as Marx pointed out in the *Critique of the Gotha Programme*, and then what remains will be divided among the 'civilized co-operators' in the form of dividends so that the 'civilized co-operators', as the expression of the working class in terms of socialist relations of production, benefit from the wealth that they have created. Through 'co-operative labour' the civilized-co-operators' will engage in tasks, as Lenin pointed out, such as the abolition of classes and the ending of the exploitation of man by man during the period of the 'dictatorship of the proletariat' in the 'building of socialism'.

Conclusion

There has to be debate and discussion on exactly what is the system of socialism. For too long the International Communist Movement, the International Left has peddled the notion that the system of socialism is based on 'state ownership' or 'public ownership' or 'socialist public ownership'. It is the task of Scientific Socialism to dispel such an erroneous conception.

Essay 3: The philosophy of socialist humanity

In the twentieth century, socialism came to the fore to challenge capitalism. The first socialist revolution was the Great October Revolution of 1917 led by Lenin and the Bolsheviks. By 1924, just before his death, Lenin wrote that the 'system of civilized co-operators is the system of socialism' in his article 'On Co-operation'.

Stalin, when he took over the helm of Soviet socialism, did not fully develop the co-operative system as the system of Soviet socialism. He took it on the path of the 'state monopoly system' based on 'state ownership' or 'public ownership' of the means of production as the dominant expression of property relations under socialism. This led to the 'State', led by the Communist Party of the Soviet Union (CPSU), dominating all aspects of Soviet life. In the 1950s, there developed 'Marxism-Leninism' to justify the 'state-monopoly system' in the Soviet Union and the socialist countries of Eastern Europe which followed the Soviet 'model' of socialist development. At first, the 'state monopoly system' showed itself as being successful based on the 'enthusiasm' (Lenin's word) of the working people of the Soviet Union. By the 1970s the 'state monopoly system' began to stagnate. It was not meeting the material needs and wants of the working people of the Soviet Union. By the late 1980s there was a crisis in Soviet Socialism during the era of Gorbachev between those who advocated 'state monopoly' and those who advocated the 'co-operative system'. For those who advocated 'state monopoly' the 'co-operative system' smelt too much of capitalism. The battle between these two opposing sides led to the demise of the CPSU and the implosion of Soviet socialism. At the same time, the countries of Eastern Europe like Poland and others began to reject the Soviet 'model' of socialism. These countries turned to capitalism.

Lenin stated that history moves in a 'zigzag'. The history of socialism shows that socialism in the twentieth century moved in a 'zigzag'. The implosion of the Soviet 'model' of 'state monopoly' led to a certain skepticism in 'socialism' by the working class of the world. Bourgeois ideologists crowed and declared that capitalism was in the stage of Globalization.

'Marxism-Leninism' still adheres to state ownership or public ownership of the means of production under socialism. In fact, the Communist Party of Britain (CPB), as an individual example, declares on its website, that 'public ownership' is the 'essence of socialism'. This British political organization sees 'public ownership' under capitalism, which it advocates, as leading to 'socialist public ownership' within socialism and being its 'essence'. Its position is certainly different from the position of Lenin. It is within this context that I would like to develop the 'philosophy of socialist humanity'.

It is to Marx that I turn to develop the 'philosophy of socialist humanity'. Marx in his 'Theses on Feuerbach' argues thus:

"The standpoint of the old materialism is civil society; the standpoint of the new is human society, or social humanity." (Thesis X, Karl Marx, selected writings, McLellan. D. Oxford, 2000)

Scientific Socialism is the new materialism which has to have a 'philosophy' concerning what Marx called 'social humanity'. Given the attempts to develop socialism in the twentieth century and its failures there needs to be a 'philosophy' having its roots in 'social humanity' to rekindle the drive for socialism. That 'philosophy' I call 'socialist humanity'.

The 'philosophy of socialist humanity' has to have materialist roots. It starts with being premised on the 'base' (Marx's concept). The 'economic base' of the philosophy of socialist humanity has the co-operative system as the mode of production of socialism, Marx pointed out that socialism is 'co-operative society based on common ownership'. Lenin pointed out that the 'system of civilized co-operators is the system of socialism'. These two great revolutionaries argued that the co-operative system is the mode of production of socialism.

The co-operative mode of production within the 'phase' of socialism has to have socialist 'relations of production'. For Lenin, the concept 'civilized co-operators' expressed socialist relations of production which reflected direct social ownership of the means of production by the working class with political power in its hands and those of its political representatives.

The co-operative mode of production or system expresses working class co-operation in economic activity. 'Civilized co-operators' as expression of socialist relations of production have to benefit from the functioning of the co-operative mode of production.

It is important to understand the 'ethos's' of the co-operative movement in the twenty first century. I 'googled' it on the internet and I came to a greater understanding.

There are certain co-operative values of the co-operative movement under capitalism. The first is 'self-help'. The second is 'self-responsibility'. The third is 'democracy'. The fourth is 'equality'. The fifth is 'equity' and the sixth is 'solidarity'. These values are based on co-operative principles. These principles are (1) Voluntary and Open Membership; (2) Democratic Member Control; (3) Member economic participation; (4) Autonomy and Independence and (5) Education Training and Information.

The 'purpose' of the co-operative is to 'meet the economic, social and cultural needs of their members'. It is organized on the basis of 'one member, one vote' and the 'profits' are 'reinvested in the co-operative with the remaining surplus divided among members' and their money comes from their membership, loans, among other things.

In his 'Inaugural Address to the First International', Marx had this to say:

"...We speak of the co-operative movement, especially the co-operative factories raised by the unassisted efforts of a few bold 'hands'. The value of these great social experiments cannot be over-rated. By deed, instead of by argument, they have shown that production on a large scale, and in accord with the behests of modern science, may be carried on without the existence of a class of masters employing a class of hands; that to bear fruit, the means of labour need not be monopolized as a means of domination over, and of extortion against, the laboring man himself; and that, like slave labour, like serf labour, hired labour is but a transitory and inferior form, destined to disappear before associated labour plying its toil with a willing hand, a ready mind, and a joyous heart...To save the industrious masses, co-operative labour ought to be developed to national dimensions, and consequently, to be fostered by national means." (Karl Marx, 'Selected Writings', Second Edition, 2000, Edited by D. McLellan, p. 580.)

Under socialism, the first phase of communism according to Marx, socialist co-operatives would be organized differently primarily because there is social ownership of the means of production in the hands of the working class. The co-operative is the objectification of social ownership of the means of production. The co-operative, which arises out of the womb of capitalism, under socialism and social ownership of the means of production, becomes the individual representation of the co-operative mode of production. The co-operative is the working class or proletarian organization at the level of the 'base' or economy. The workers as 'civilized co-operators', as an expression of socialist relations of production, have to be organized in co-operatives as Lenin argued. Lenin's concept 'civilized co-operators' expresses that property relation is in the hands of the workers. Lenin's concept 'civilized co-operators', as an expression of socialist relations of production, will have certain socialist values

The first is connected with 'democracy' at the level of the 'base' or the socialist economy. This means 'democratic worker control' with 'one co-operator, one vote'. This is connected to another value which is 'equality'. Lenin's concept 'civilized co-operators' expresses 'equality' irrespective of workers' race, gender, sexual attitudes, and religion. This value is connected to another that of 'equity' where at the level of the economy there is fairness and justice. 'Civilized co-operators' is an expression of 'solidarity' not simply among the workers but also in relation to the community. The relationship between 'civilized co-operators', and between 'civilized co-operators' and the community is very important in the shaping of the social structure of socialism.

'Civilized co-operators', who are engaged in 'co-operative labour' (Marx), will share in the surplus that the co-operative makes after a portion of the surplus is reinvested in the co-operative and a portion is allocated for the Social Fund on the basis of 'each according to his or her work'. This means economic benefit from social ownership of the means of production by the 'civilized co-operators' from the wealth that they created.

All these factors working together ensure that the 'civilized co-operator' is not 'alienated' (Marx's concept) from the means of production as the worker is under capitalism and as the worker was in the 'state monopoly system' in the Soviet Union and in eastern Europe. 'Civilized co-operators' expresses that the workers are at one with the means of production. 'Civilized co-operators' is an expression of the negation of 'alienation'. The co-operative mode of production, with 'civilized co-operators' expressing socialist relations of production, negates 'economic alienation' and the 'cash nexus' so dominant under capitalism. 'Co-operation' bring to the fore the 'creativity' of the worker as 'civilized co-operators', who is at one with the means of production. Lenin's concept 'civilized co-operators' develops the worker to fulfill his or her mode of life, their 'species-being' and an end to all forms of 'commodity fetishism'. 'Civilized co-operators' means not only that the workers are at one with the means of production but also in the realization of the social product through the co-operative mode of production. 'Co-operation' means the negation of alienation' as the 'civilized co-operator' fulfills his or her mode of life in relation between the individual and the universal, that is to say, society, especially at the level of the 'base'.

The most significant feature of 'civilized co-operators' is 'economic democracy'. Under capitalism there is no economic democracy for the worker. Power is in the hands of the capitalist. Under socialism, through economic democracy with 'one co-operator, one vote', there is an end to exploitation and shows that the 'civilized co-operators' are masters of economic activity under socialism. Through economic democracy based on social ownership of the means of production there is the expression of the 'dictatorship of the proletariat'. Economic democracy through 'one co-operator', one vote' is very important for the expression of the 'dictatorship of the proletariat' at the level of the base. The 'dictatorship of the proletariat' is expressed through economic democracy not through 'force'. Through economic democracy which expresses the 'dictatorship of the proletariat' there is the functioning of 'socialist democracy' at the level of the 'base'. Economic democracy means economic empowerment of the 'civilized co-operators'.

The second significant feature is 'co-operation'. Economic co-operation among the 'civilized co-operators', based on economic democracy would slowly lead to the beginning of the end of the division of labour. Through 'co-operation' the many become the one. Through 'co-operation' there is the negation of capitalist greed and there develops a positivity for 'socialist labour' or as Marx called it 'co-operative labour'. Through 'co-operative labour', 'civilized co-operators' ensure the functioning of socialism. Marx pointed out in *Capital*, Vol.1, page 313, that:

"All combined labour on a large scale requires, more or less, a directing authority, in order to secure the harmonious working of the individual activities, and to perform the general functions that have their origin in the action of the combined organism."

This general statement by Marx on 'Co-operation' is very applicable to the co-operative mode of production of socialism. At the primary level of the co-operative, the 'civilized co-operators' through 'economic democracy' will elect a board to ensure the 'harmonious working' of the co-operative. The next level could be the election of regional co-operative boards with delegates from the local co-operatives and finally there is the national co-operative body elected by regional boards with delegates elected from regional boards that will be engaged in economic central planning.

Through 'Co-operation' in the first phase of communism, that is, socialism, through 'co-operative labour', the 'civilized co-operators' will be engaged in the building of socialism, and will also be engaged in the abolition of all classes, and ending the exploitation of man by man as Lenin pointed out.

In the first phase of communism, that is, socialism, there will be co-operatives that will be premised on concentration or 'reproduction on an extended scale' (Marx) and centralization through the attraction of co-operatives to each other. The economic laws of concentration and centralization will prevail and determine the socialist economy. The law of centralization is very important for small and medium co-operatives because it will enable these socialist enterprises to become large co-operatives. Large co-operatives will try to attract small or medium co-operatives to themselves which prepare the way for the higher phase, that of communism. Centralization and concentration will be the nucleus of socialist accumulation.

Modern Science and technological developments within socialism will greatly aid the relationship between the 'civilized co-operators' and machinery gradually allowing the former to engage in the 'administration of things' (Marx) in the higher phase of communism.

The co-operative mode of production, the system of socialism, thus provides economic well-being. It meets the needs and wants of 'civilized co-operators' who would engage in a socialist 'market' which is dominated by 'retail' co-operatives. The socialist 'market' provides an outlet for the realization of the products of co-operatives. The socialist 'market' will gradually 'wither away', like the State, as socialism develops into the higher phase, communism.

Economic co-operation in the form of the co-operative mode of production allows the 'civilized co-operators', as expression of socialist relations of production, to develop, at the level of the base, the economic moral, the 'socialist good'. The 'socialist good', at the level of the base, expresses the situation that socialism meets the needs and wants of 'civilized co-operators' through material incentives like dividends from the surplus produced by the co-operative. The co-operative mode of production, through 'civilized co-operators', is engaged in the development of the 'socialist good'.

The 'socialist good' as an economic morality, is an expression of the negation of exploitation from the mode of production. This is the new in the co-operative system as the mode of production of socialism. The 'socialist good' at the level of the 'base' expresses the economic and material well-being of the 'civilized co-operators'. The 'socialist good' expresses 'co-operation' as vital in serving the material well-being of the working class or the 'civilized co-operators'. 'Co-operation', on the other hand, leads to the development of the 'socialist good' as the 'essence' of socialism through 'co-operative values'. This is completely and absolutely different from capitalism which has no morality in the exploitation of the workers for profits.

The 'socialist good', which is expressed at the level of the 'base', negates capitalist greed, envy, jealously and propagates through co-operation a new economic morality. Capitalism's end and aim is profits based on 'individualism'. In contrast the 'socialist good' seeks the balance between the 'civilized co-operator', the individual worker, and sociality through the co-operative system. No two co-operators are the same. Each will contribute his/her 'co-operative labour' and obtain the requisite rewards. Marx makes this point in the *Critique of the Gotha Programme*. Through 'co-operative labour', as an expression of the 'socialist good', there is the reproduction and functioning of socialism.

The co-operative mode of production, like no other mode of production before it, including 'primitive communalism' (Marx), defines the 'socialist good' as in the interests of the dictatorship of the proletariat. This can be clearly seen in the workings of economic democracy through 'one co-operator, one vote'. 'Economic democracy' through 'one co-operator, one vote', expressing the 'socialist good' shows clearly that the 'dictatorship of the proletariat' under socialism is a democratic one. Economic empowerment of the 'civilized co-operators' defines the 'socialist good' as this social moral expresses the 'dictatorship of the proletariat'.

The 'socialist good', given its expression at the level of the 'base', is a negation of the alienation that the worker, individually speaking, and the working class in general lives through within the capitalist mode of production. The 'socialist good at the level of the 'base' expresses the fulfillment of both the individual, the 'civilized co-operator', and the whole, that is, society. 'Civilized co-operators' engaged in 'co-operative labour' express the 'socialist good' which is a negation of 'alienation'. 'Social humanity' (Marx) comes to the fore.

'Civilized co-operators' engaged in the co-operative mode of production through 'co-operation' express 'social humanity', which is a new phenomenon in human development. 'Co-operative labour' is a new expression of 'social humanity' at the level of the 'base'. 'Co-operative labour' which reflects the 'socialist good' is an expression of the new phenomenon 'social humanity'. The socio-economic culture of co-operatives which is shown through Lenin's concept 'civilized co-operators' as socialist relations of production expresses the new phenomenon 'social humanity'.

The 'dictatorship of the proletariat' as represented by the co-operative mode of production and 'civilized co-operators' as the relations of production in the phase of socialism expresses 'socialist humanity'. It is clear that the 'dictatorship of the proletariat' cannot be viewed through 'force' as Lenin pointed out. The 'dictatorship of the proletariat' has to be viewed through 'economic democracy' in the form of 'one co-operator, one vote' as this expresses social ownership of the means of production with political power in the hands of the working class.

At the level of the socialist 'base' there is the expression of socialist humanity. The first phase of communist society, that is, socialism, at the level of the 'base', cannot but express 'socialist humanity'. This is the new in the transition from capitalism to communism especially its first phase, socialism.

The co-operative mode of production is the 'business' system of the working class, of socialism, just as capitalist mode of production is the business system of the capitalists. The co-operative mode of production negates wage labour through the development of 'co-operative labour'.

I would like to digress and discuss, briefly, the position of 'Marxism-Leninism' and the Communist Party of Britain (CPB). I have, at the beginning, mentioned that this ideology and the CPB, which defends this ideology, advocate 'public ownership'. In the CPB case, it sees 'public ownership' as the '...essence of socialism'.

'Public ownership', under socialism, is 'state ownership' of the means of production through socialist nationalization. It leads to the ownership and control of the means of production by the State and results in the formation of the 'state monopoly' system. The 'state monopoly' system was the basis of Soviet socialism in the Soviet Union. It failed because there was an absence of socialist relations of production which led to the alienation of the workers from the means of production according to the late Joe Slovo of the South African Communist Party (SACP). Lenin, when he discussed 'war communism' and the state monopoly system that developed had this to say:

"Theoretically speaking, state monopoly is not necessarily the best system from the standpoint of the interests of socialism." (Selected Works, Volume 3, p.517, Progress)

In the early 1990s when the 'state monopoly' system of the Soviet Union imploded, it did so because the Communist Party of the Soviet Union could no longer rely on the 'enthusiasm of the working people' and that the 'state monopoly' system failed to meet the needs and wants of the Soviet peoples'.

Yet 'Marxism-Leninism' in general and the CPB in particular still cling on to the position that 'public ownership' and the system that arises, that of 'state monopoly', is the 'essence' of socialism. 'Marxism-Leninism', as an ideology, was developed in the Soviet Union to justify the 'state monopoly' system that Stalin set up from the 1930s onwards through 'state ownership' of the means of production. There is a stark contrast, nay, contradiction, between 'Marxism-Leninism' which advocates 'public ownership' and the position of Scientific Socialism as represented by Marx and Lenin who advocated the co-operative system as the system of socialism.

I have discussed this in a previous chapter and cannot go into great detail here. It is important to note that 'Marxism-Leninism' sees public ownership' of the means of production as the dominant expression of socialist property relations under socialism whilst the co-operative system is accorded a secondary and subordinate role. In the case of the CPB, 'public ownership' of the means of production not only expresses dominant property relations within socialism but is also its 'essence'. The CPB analysis on the Soviet Union shows that it is blind to Lenin's concept 'state monopoly'. The CPB talks about a 'bureaucratic-command system' that existed in the Soviet Union. This is reminiscent of Trotsky's analysis of the Soviet Union. Trotsky, similarly, was blind to Lenin's concept 'state monopoly'.

Secondly, the system of 'state monopoly' that arises out of 'public ownership' of the means of production could not develop any kind of philosophy of socialist humanity at the level of the 'base' because of the dominance of the 'State' in economic life in the Soviet Union. From 'state ownership' to socialist nationalization of the means of production leading to the formation of state enterprises which results in the workers under socialism being treated as 'state employees'. This was the case in the Soviet Union. The 'state monopoly' system turns the workers into 'state employees'. 'State employees' are not an expression of socialist relations of production. It appears that the CPB, by advocating 'public ownership' or 'state ownership', is following the Soviet 'model' or system which led to the State dominating economic life. The 'State' stood over and above the workers. This was the experience of the 'state monopoly' system in the Soviet Union where 'State central planning' led by the Communist Party of the Soviet Union (CPSU) dominated. In this sense, the peculiarity of the 'state monopoly' system was that it meant that 'politics determined economics'. The economic 'base', given 'state monopoly', was practically non-existent. The Lada cars produced in the Soviet Union were regarded as a joke, for example. The 'state monopoly' system in the Soviet Union was only good for military and space technology. The 'state monopoly' system in the Soviet Union did not prove that socialism was a higher mode of production than capitalism. It was not socialism that failed but that the 'state monopoly' system in the Soviet Union showed itself as not in the interests of socialism. 'Public ownership', which the CPB advocates, shows itself, given the experience of the Soviet Union, as not in the interests of socialism. The CPB position is 'Stalinism' dressed-up as 'Marxism-Leninism' and is untenable. It is untenable because the 'state monopoly' system and the co-operative system are two different systems that are incompatible within socialism. They cannot co-exist within the stage of socialism. This was the case in the Soviet Union from Stalin onwards where Stalin did not persevere with Lenin's recommendation of organizing the workers in co-operatives which would take a whole epoch. Stalin developed the 'state monopoly' system based on 'state ownership' which after a few decades ousted the co-operative system as the dominant expression of socialist property relations. The development of the 'state monopoly' system, which came to be regarded as representing socialism by Soviet 'Marxist-Leninists' and the International Communist Movement, and the 'contradictions' that arose led to the downfall of Soviet socialism.

Marx argued that socialism is 'co-operative society' based on 'common ownership'. Lenin argued that the 'system of civilized co-operators is the system of socialism. Lenin was aware of 'state monopoly' as expressed in 'War Communism' and rejected it by developing the New Economic Policy which, just before his untimely death, he later transformed it to the development of the co-operative system as the system of socialism.

The co-operative system is the mode of production of socialism. This is the only logical conclusion that is to be reached from the works of Marx and Lenin on the subject matter. The experience of 'Socialism' in the twentieth century and the twenty first century has shown that the co-operative system has not been developed fully as the system of socialism.

It should be clear that the co-operative system as the mode of production of socialism has an 'ethos' to it. The 'state monopoly' system, given the experience of the Soviet Union and the Eastern European countries, did not have any kind of 'ethos' and philosophy to it. This is the lesson to be learned from twentieth century experience of socialism.

It is important to understand the reasoning of the 'Marxist-Leninist' Communist Party of Britain (CPB). The CPB rationalizes that 'public ownership' under capitalism expresses some form of socialism. The CPB advocates 'public ownership' of gas, electricity, water and transport industries among others under capitalism in Britain at present, which 'Thatcherism' did away with, to counter monopoly capital domination and exploitation. This leads to the CPB, with a 'qualitative leap', to the conclusion that in the first phase of communism, that is, socialism, 'public ownership' is the 'essence of socialism'. For the CPB, 'public ownership' arises out of the womb of capitalism and becomes the 'essence' of socialism. In contrast, for Marx and Lenin, co-operative society arises out of the womb of capitalism and becomes the mode of production and the system of socialism. The 'Marxist-Leninist' CPB position is totally different from the position of Marx and Lenin. The 'Marxist-Leninist' CPB is doing a disservice to the working class when it advocates 'public ownership' as the 'essence of socialism' Such is the predilection for 'public ownership' by the CPB, that one of its leading lights, Mary Davis, argues that 'socialist public ownership' puts an end to capitalist exploitation. Mary Davis is either ignorant or unaware or does not understand Lenin's statement that 'the system of civilized co-operators is the system of socialism'.

I return to the 'philosophy of socialist humanity' which advocates the co-operative system as the system of socialism, as the mode of production of socialism. Lenin argued that 'economics determine politics'. It is on the basis of the co-operative system as the system or mode of production of socialism that we can see how it is reflected and represented at the level of the 'superstructure'.

The first point to note is that legal relations in socialist society will reflect and represent social ownership and the co-operative property form based on socialist relations of production, that of 'civilized co-operators'. The rights of 'civilized co-operators' must be enshrined in the legal relations of socialist society. The specific form that this takes will depend on objective and subjective factors.

The second point to note is that at the level of the political 'superstructure' there will be the 'dictatorship of the proletariat' which will reflect and represent the economic democracy that emanates from the 'base', the co-operative mode of production. In this sense, Lenin was correct to point out that the 'dictatorship of the proletariat' cannot be viewed through 'force'. Lenin argued that the resistance of the exploiters, the capitalists and their lackeys must be crushed but he said this:

"But the essence of proletarian dictatorship is not in force alone, or even mainly in force. Its chief feature is the organization and discipline of the advanced contingent of the working people, of their vanguard; of their sole leader, the proletariat, whose object is to build socialism, abolish the division of society into classes, make all members of society working

people and remove the basis for all exploitation of man by man." (Greetings to the Hungarian Workers, Selected Works, Vol. 3, p.161).

Lenin, in the above 'Letter' talked about the 'dictatorship of the proletariat' in the 'transition period' from capitalism to socialism. Under socialism, the 'dictatorship of the proletariat' at the level of the 'base', through the system of 'civilized co-operators' and the economic democracy that arises, will be reflected and represented in a system of socialist democracy, a political system, that would ensure that the working class, the proletariat, is engaged in the above tasks. The political system that arises depends on the objective and subjective conditions. It may be that one political party would represent 'civilized co-operators' when they are engaged in the above tasks. It is also possible that there could be many workers' parties that vie to represent 'civilized co-operators' at the level of the political 'superstructure'.

It is clear that the political system that arises as an expression of socialist democracy, will have to represent the proletariat organized as 'civilized co-operators', given that the co-operative mode of production is the system of socialism as argued by Lenin. Socialist democracy as the expression of the 'dictatorship of the proletariat' in general within socialist society, based on the co-operative mode of production, would be represented by the socialist State which is to be an enabler and facilitator in the tasks proposed by Lenin. In his article on 'On Co-operation' Lenin accords the State with a 'supervisory role' in the development of the 'system of civilized co-operators'. Lenin did not accord the State, in his article, an all-embracing, omnipotent role in the building of socialism as 'Marxism-Leninism' does through the system of 'state-monopoly' that arises from 'public ownership' or 'state ownership' as in the Soviet Union from Stalin onwards. With the system of 'civilized co-operators' as the 'system of socialism' and the socialist democracy that arises, Lenin's statement that 'politics is the concentrated expression of economics' comes to the fore. The political 'superstructure' under socialism will have to reflect and represent, or as Lenin argued 'expression of...' the economic 'base', the co-operative mode of production and the 'system of civilized co-operators' as socialist relations of production.

It is important to understand the role of the socialist State. 'Marxism-Leninism' through 'public ownership' or 'state ownership' resulting in the 'state monopoly' system can only call for the 'strengthening' of the State. In this relation, 'Marxism-Leninism' follows Stalin who called for the 'strengthening' of the State as an expression of the 'dictatorship of the proletariat' when he was engaged in developing the 'state monopoly' system in the USSR.

The philosophy of socialist humanity argues, that with the co-operative system as the system of socialism, with 'civilized co-operators' as expressing socialist relation of production, the task of a functional socialist State is to protect and defend the interests of 'civilized co-operators' who express the 'dictatorship of the proletariat' as Lenin defined it above.

This means that the State, which in the Soviet Union was the driving force of socialism and became all-powerful and dominant with the Communist Party of the Soviet Union leading it, becomes subordinate to socialist relations of production in the form of 'civilized co-operators' and exist to defend their interests, their class rule. The State will also act as an enabler, facilitator and provider in furthering the interests of 'civilized co-operators'. The State role is not to act as an 'economic agent' that dominates the socialist economy as happened in the Soviet Union through the 'state monopoly' system. The role of the State is to ensure the smooth functioning of the co-operative system as the system of socialism. In a 'theoretical' sense, from the 'materialist base', the co-operative mode of production, there would arise a socialist superstructure, including the Socialist State, which would react back on the 'base', with 'relative autonomy', in the functioning and reinforcement of socialist civil society based on 'co-operation'.

The political 'superstructure' would have a democratic electoral system that will reflect and represent the economic democracy of the 'system of civilized co-operators' at the level of the 'base' or the socialist mode of production, the co-operative system.

As socialism matures and approaches the higher phase, communism, the State will 'wither away' as the working class in the form of civilized co-operators' abolish all forms of exploitation and classes. It is not the 'strengthening' of the State as 'Marxism-Leninism' calls for through 'public ownership', which results in 'state monopoly', but to 'strengthen' socialist relations of production, 'civilized co-operators', as expression of the 'dictatorship of the proletariat' who are engaged in building socialism.

 The third point to note is that 'socialist morality' would take the best of 'bourgeois morality', including 'human rights', and be developed on the basis of co-operation, and the end of 'all exploitation of man by man', this should be the basis of socialism. The development of 'socialist morality' will be led by the proletariat as 'civilized co-operators', the vanguard of all working people. Socialist morality, given the existence of the co-operative mode of production, would be concerned with 'fairness' and 'justice', for want of a better word 'equity' and lead to the negation of 'greed' and 'inequality' that is so prevalent in bourgeois society. 'Co-operation' becomes the basis of socialist morality within socialist civil society. Socialist morality would have, at its core, the 'socialist good' which has its origins in the co-operative mode of production, in 'co-operative values' and expresses itself as 'socialist consciousness'.

Socialist morality will have its expression in legal relations which would represent the interests of the 'civilized co-operators', the proletariat vanguard, and all working people. Socialist morality and socialist legal relations are inter-linked and express how socialist civil society functions on the basis of 'co-operation'. In this sense, there is the determination of what Marx called 'co-operative society'. Socialist morality will develop in accordance with the development of the 'materialist base', the co-operative mode of production. It is not a question of 'economic determinism' but the dialectical interaction between the 'materialist base' and socialist morality with socialist morality reinforcing the 'co-operative values' at the level of the base and in this sense, socialist morality would have a certain 'relative autonomy'. Socialist civil society thus functions not only in relation to the 'economic base', the co-operative mode of production, but will also be guided by socialist morality encompassing 'co-operative values'.

The 'co-operative values' that develop at the 'materialist base', through the co-operative mode of production, will have its reflection and representation through legal relations, socialist morality, the political superstructure, in socialist consciousness. Socialist consciousness arises from socialist being through the cooperative mode of production. It leads to the development of the 'socialist human being' who is all-rounded in his/her approach. This is the 'essence' of what Marx called 'social humanity' or 'socialist humanity'. It is not, as the Communist Party of Britain claims, that 'public ownership' is the 'essence' of socialism.

Without the first phase of socialism as 'co-operative society', on the basis of 'common ownership' there cannot come into being communism, communist society. I digress slightly to say that the system of 'state monopoly' that arose in the Soviet Union, from Stalin onwards and to the 1980s, through 'state ownership' or 'public ownership' did not lead to and cannot lead to communism. This is what the 'Marxist-Leninist' Communist Party of Britain fails to understand when it avers that 'public ownership' is the 'essence' of socialism. 'Public ownership' does not lead to communism and this can be seen in practice in the Soviet Union. For 'Marxism-Leninism' in general and in the individual organization, the Communist Party of Britain, that 'public ownership' is the 'essence' of socialism is a political delusion that differs from the concreteness of the positions of Marx and Lenin on this issue.

It is the system of 'civilized co-operators', as Lenin pointed out, in the first phase, socialism, that will pave the way to communism. The 'civilized co-operators' in the first phase, socialism, will be engaged in the abolition of classes, the end of the exploitation of man by man, the ending of division of labour and the division of the sexes, the development of socialist humanity, the development of the all-rounded 'socialist human being', in a phrase 'the building of socialism', that will pave the way to communism.

I write this essay as 'food for thought' and discussion so as to ascertain what is the system of socialism. 'Marxism-Leninism' avers that 'public ownership' is the system of socialism, nay, and the 'essence' of socialism. It leads to the system of 'state monopoly' which in the Soviet Union showed itself as not in the interests of the working class and all working people when it imploded. The system of 'civilized co-operators', the co-operative system, has not been fully developed in the history of socialism in the twentieth century and in the twenty first century. Objective and subjective conditions may be responsible for this lack of development of the co-operative system as the 'system of socialism' but the main problem has been 'Marxism-Leninism' *obsession* with 'public ownership' or 'state ownership' and the 'state monopoly' system that arises from such a development. It leads to, as in the Soviet Union and in the former Eastern European 'socialist' countries, to the 'alienation' of the working people in general and the working class from the means of production.

The philosophy of socialist humanity is concerned with the socialist 'good' that is an expression of socialist consciousness that has its basis in 'co-operative values'. The ethos and philosophy of co-operation, at the level of the base and at the level of the ideological superstructure, represents 'socialist humanity'. The 'philosophy of socialist humanity' is concerned with overcoming the 'alienation' that developed in countries that adopted the Soviet 'model', the 'state monopoly' system.

This is a philosophy of a new type that expresses the advances that the 'socialist human being' has made whilst developing socialism and paving the way for the transition to communism. It has to be developed by many hands that are interested and engaged in the building of socialism. I only discuss the basic rudiments drawn from the 'materialist base', the co-operative mode of production, as the system of socialism, as Marx and Lenin argued.

Context of the essays

I shall conclude first with the essays on socialism and then finally discuss 'Globalization'.

The essay on the 'state monopoly' system in the Soviet Union was first investigated in 1993. I returned to it next in 2005 and then finally finished it between 2011 and 2014.

The concept 'state monopoly' is, as I have mentioned, Lenin's concept which he used to characterize the period of 'War Communism'. Stalin, when he took over the helm of Soviet socialism and first formulated 'Leninism' and also, developed 'state ownership' or 'public ownership' as the dominant property relations in the Soviet Union from the 1930s onwards. This led to the development of the 'state monopoly' system in the Soviet Union which lasted until the implosion of the Soviet Union in the early 1990s.

It was through this historical process that 'Marxism-Leninism' became the dominant ideology of the International Communist Movement and usurped Scientific Socialism. There is no principle within Scientific Socialism that states that 'state' or 'public' ownership is the 'essence of socialism' as the Communist Party of Britain claims. Both Marx and Lenin advocated the co-operative system as the system of socialism. The system of 'state monopoly' as the system of socialism, based on 'state ownership' or 'public ownership' of the means of production, has their root in 'Stalinism' which later became known as 'Marxism-Leninism'.   Ever since then, the International Communist Movement, which adopted 'Marxism-Leninism' as its ideology, has advocated 'state' or 'public' ownership leading to the system of 'state monopoly' as the 'essence' of socialism. This is clear in the positions of the Communist Party of Britain (CPB) and the South African Communist Party (SACP).

In writing the essay on the 'state monopoly' system of the Soviet Union I became clarified that 'Marxism-Leninism' and Scientific Socialism were not the same. This is clear on what is the system of socialism. 'Marxism-Leninism's' advocacy of 'state' or 'public' ownership leading to 'state monopoly' has been shown, through historical events in the late 1980s and early 1990s, not to be in the interests of the working class. 'Marxism-Leninism', by clinging on to 'state ownership' or 'public ownership' which leads to 'state monopoly', shows itself as Stalinist dogma. 'Marxism-Leninism' is, thus, nothing else than 'Stalinism in disguise' in regards to the question of socialism. This is not Lenin's position. If there is such an ideology as 'Leninism', which Stalin developed to justify his rule, it should be argued that the 'system of civilized co-operators' is the system of socialism as Lenin argued. 'State' or 'public' ownership leading to the 'state monopoly' system as the system of socialism is not 'Leninism' but 'Stalinism'. 'Marxism-Leninism' fails to pay heed to Lenin's position on the system of socialism. Instead it parrots that 'state' or 'public' ownership leading to 'state monopoly' is 'Leninism' which is an erroneous position and does Lenin a disservice. Mary Davis, one of the leading lights of the Communist Party of Britain (CPB), does Lenin a disservice by her advocacy of 'socialist public ownership'. 'Socialist public ownership' is certainly not Lenin's position. It is not the position of Marx either. Whose position is it within the history of the international working class movement? It belongs to Stalin. 'Socialist public ownership' has its roots in 'Stalinism'. Mary Davis, who sees herself as a 'Marxist-Leninist,' is nothing more than a 'Stalinist in disguise'. Her organization, the CPB, states that 'public ownership' is the 'essence' of socialism, is nothing else than 'Stalinism in disguise'. *Objectively*, they are 'Stalinists'.

Lenin's concept 'state monopoly' has not previously been used to characterize the system that existed in the Soviet Union for approximately sixty years. Lenin's concept 'state monopoly' is the only concept that accurately depicts the Soviet 'model'. I contrast it to the CPB notion that a 'bureaucratic-command system' developed in the Soviet Union. As I have mentioned previously, the CPB notion is close to Trotskyism. Furthermore, with this notion, the CPB does not begin its analysis on a materialist basis. Moreover, it is a denial of the fact that 'public or state ownership' is not the system of socialism. The 'Marxist-Leninist' CPB notion of a 'bureaucratic-command system' preserves 'public or state ownership' as the system of socialism whilst blaming the implosion of Soviet socialism on the domination of a socialist 'bureaucracy' led by the Communist Party of the Soviet Union and a lack of democratic accountability. The CPB fails to realize that the 'state monopoly' system that arises out of 'public' or 'state ownership' means that there is a 'top- down approach' to the building of socialism. In practice, it means that the working class is not engaged in the building of socialism and becomes alienated from the means of production as happened in the Soviet Union. Finally, there is the absence of discussion on 'relations of production' in the Soviet Union. 'Marxism-Leninism' has a habit of not discussing 'relations of production' under socialism from my investigations. There is an objective reason why this is the case. The call for 'public or state ownership' as the system of socialism, as the 'essence' of socialism necessitates the negation of 'socialist relations of production'. This is precisely what the CPB notion 'bureaucratic-command system' does. The CPB position is a 'gut reaction' rather than a Scientific Socialist position.

It is clear that apart from its avowal of 'public ownership' both within capitalism and in the phase of socialism the CPB is clueless on the system of socialism. 'Public ownership' or 'state ownership' is the mantra of the CPB by which it 'dupes' the working class as to what socialism constitutes or is based on. A communist organization which calls itself a communist party as the CPB does must develop the concept of socialism and its system and the CPB has patently failed to do so for the working class to be politically educated on the transformation from capitalism to socialism. This is the 'reality' of British communism which 'believes' in 'public ownership' or 'state ownership'. The problem with Slovo and the SACP analysis titled 'Has Socialism Failed?' is that Slovo talks about 'existing socialism' but fails to explain what was the system of 'existing socialism' in the Soviet Union and the East European countries, the socialist 'bloc'. I endeavored to find the system of 'existing socialism' and came to the conclusion that it was the 'state monopoly system' which led to an 'absence of socialist relations of production' and the 'alienation' of the working class from the means of production within the Soviet Union. This was the only logical way to explain the implosion of Soviet socialism.

I turn to the 'philosophy of socialist humanity'. In 2010 I was 're-reading' Marx's 'Theses on Feuerbach' and I was attracted to the thesis on 'social humanity'. Since the implosion of the Soviet Union, socialism has had 'bad publicity'. I decided to take up Marx's challenge. At first I investigated purely from a one-sided 'philosophical' approach. Then in late 2011 I realized that Scientific Socialism is a materialist philosophy and therefore a 'philosophy of socialist humanity' must begin from materialist premises, from the economic base. The economic base was the co-operative system as it was clear that 'state monopoly' based on 'public ownership' or 'state ownership' is not the system of socialism.

As I researched the co-operative system, I came to the conclusion that this economic system has its own 'philosophy' based on 'economic co-operation'. Capitalism as an economic system does not have an economic 'philosophy' apart from the profit motive. In contrast, the co-operative system develops the economic philosophy of 'economic co-operation'. This is reflected in the ideological superstructure especially at the levels of politics and socialist morality. One man or woman cannot espouse a full 'philosophy of socialist humanity'. It has to be the work of many who are willing to contribute to the debate on socialism and what is the system of socialism. It is clear that the 'state monopoly' system based on 'public' ownership has no philosophy or ethos to it and cannot capture the socialist 'imagination' of the working class. 'State monopoly' based on 'public ownership' is 'alienated' property relations which is what happened in the Soviet Union during the period of its implosion. The CPB 'idea' that 'public ownership' is the 'essence' of socialism is erroneous and is 'Marxism-Leninism' peddling its dogma. History has done away with this dogma peddled by 'Marxism-Leninism' but the problem is that 'Marxist-Leninist' organizations like the CPB and the SACP are still peddling the dogma that 'public ownership' is the 'essence' of socialism.

In writing this conclusion, I did not start out with the intention of writing a critique of 'Marxism-Leninism'. My first intention was to discover the system of socialism as advocated by Marx and Lenin. As I have mentioned, Marx and Lenin propagated the co-operative system as the system of socialism. In contrast, 'Marxism-Leninism', having its roots in 'Stalinism', peddles the dogma that 'public ownership' is the 'essence' of socialism. This contrast became clear to me during my investigations on the subject matter of 'what is the system of socialism'? It became clear to me through my investigations, especially after the death of Lenin and from Stalin onwards, there developed the system of 'state monopoly' based on 'public ownership' or 'state ownership' being the dominant expression of property relations within socialism in the twentieth century. The history of the late twentieth century shows that this system of 'state monopoly' based on 'public ownership' or 'state ownership' failed and imploded because it did not meet the wants and needs of the working class and its socialist 'philosophy'. Given that Stalin maintained Lenin's position of 'socialism in one country' he did so on an erroneous system, that of 'state monopoly' based on 'state or public ownership', and did not take into account fully Lenin's statement that 'the system of civilized co-operators is the system of socialism', that the co-operative system is the system of socialism. This is one of Stalin 'sins'.

Furthermore, the question arises: why is 'Marxism-Leninism' so enamoured with 'public ownership'? This is because it enables *state control* of the economy and society by the ruling communist party as developed in the Soviet Union with the Communist Party of the Soviet Union from Stalin onwards. 'State monopoly' based on 'state or public ownership' leads to state control, which negates the economic democracy that the co-operative system propagates, as developed in the Soviet Union from Stalin onwards.

The main objective of developing a 'philosophy of socialist humanity' based on the co-operative system is to overcome the 'alienation' that the working class of the Soviet Union experienced, as argued by the late Joe Slovo of the South African Communist Party, due to the 'state monopoly' system of the Soviet Union.

Socialism is concerned with the negation of 'alienation' that the working class experiences under capitalism. Given 'social' or common ownership' of the means of production, the working class under socialism is at one with the means of production. It is important to note that when 'state' or 'public' ownership becomes the norm in socialist society which transpired in the Soviet Union from Stalin onwards, it initially was greeted with the enthusiasm of the working class. As it developed, it led to growth but by the 1970s and 80s the 'state monopoly' system based on 'public' ownership or 'state ownership' began to stagnate and was falling behind capitalism in terms of development. The late Joe Slovo argued that there was an 'absence' of socialist relations of production in the Soviet Union which led to the working class becoming 'alienated' from the means of production. Slovo does not talk about the 'system' or 'model' of Soviet socialism which resulted in the absence of socialist relations of production and the alienation of working people. Slovo does not analyze the 'system' in the Soviet Union. This makes his analysis weak. I decided to work out the 'system' in the Soviet Union from works by Soviet 'Marxism-Leninism'. From my investigations I came to the conclusion that a 'system' based on 'public' or 'state ownership' leads to 'state monopoly' which is Lenin's concept. Lenin argued that the system of 'state monopoly' is not necessarily the best system from the viewpoint of the interests of socialism. The system of 'state monopoly' based on 'public' or 'state' ownership that developed in the Soviet Union from Stalin onwards which dominated Soviet society and subordinated co-operative property relations meant that there was no 'real' socialist economy. This led to an absence of socialist relations of production and 'alienation' of the working class from the means of production because of state dominance of the 'economy' through 'state industries' and 'state enterprises' and 'state central planning'. The system of 'state monopoly' based on 'public' or 'state ownership' led to the development of a 'socialist bureaucracy' dominated by the Communist Party of the Soviet Union (CPSU).

Given the demise of the Soviet Union, given the demise of the 'state monopoly' system based on 'state' or 'public' ownership, the Communist Party of Britain and its sister organizations cannot argue that 'public ownership' is the 'essence' of socialism. The experience of the Soviet Union shows that the 'Marxist-Leninist' Communist Party of Britain's statement that 'public ownership' is the 'essence' of socialism is erroneous and propagating such a notion is misleading the working class in Britain as to what the system of socialism actually is according to Marx and Lenin. The 'Marxist-Leninist' Communist Party of Britain is ignorant of Lenin's concept of 'state monopoly' and is reluctant to talk about the 'state monopoly system' that existed in the Soviet Union based on 'public' or 'state' ownership because this would negate its position that 'public ownership' is the 'essence' of socialism.

The 'philosophy of socialist humanity' is an attempt to overcome the 'alienation' that the 'state monopoly' system exudes. It is an attempt to show that Lenin's concept 'civilized co-operators' expresses, correctly, socialist relations of production. It is an attempt to show that 'civilized co-operators' engaged in economic 'co-operation' will develop an ideological superstructure including the 'State' that will be commensurate or 'corresponds' with the economic base. The 'philosophy of socialist humanity' follows Marx in that socialism which is 'co-operative society based on common ownership' is the first phase of communism. The first phase, that is socialism, based on 'co-operation', is necessary for the transition to communism proper. In contrast, the 'Marxist-Leninist' Communist Party of Britain statement that 'public ownership' is the 'essence' of socialism does not 'correspond' with the principles of Scientific Socialism on socialism as developed by Marx and Lenin. The conclusion has to be reached that on the question of the 'first phase', socialism, 'Marxism-Leninism' is nothing else than 'Stalinism in disguise'.

I turn to the essay on 'Globalization'. As I have mentioned in the essay I began research in 2001 and completed my investigations in 2006 when I published the results on my website, global messenger.webs.com.

The aftermath of the implosion of the Soviet Union and the disbanding of the Communist Party of the Soviet Union in the early 1990s saw bourgeois ideologists crow that capitalism had changed. Some wrote theories of capitalism and its history in a subjective rather than in an objective manner. A very few took a more intelligent approach and I used them where appropriate. The 'intelligent' bourgeois ideologists made me aware of the growing trend in capitalist economic integration: the classical expression is the European Union. Nowhere in the world has capitalist economic integration reached such a high stage as in Europe. This trend cannot be reversed unless capitalism collapses into anarchy not socialism because socialism will use this development of economic integration in its interest.

This trend of capitalist economic integration could not be sited within Lenin's theory of Imperialism. In fact, 'Marxism-Leninism' is, practically, silent on the question of this growing trend of capitalist economic integration which is a new development of capitalism in its mature epoch. The only source I could turn to was Soviet 'Marxism-Leninism' from the 1980s they talked about 'Imperialist integration'. I researched this 'notion' from the viewpoint of Lenin's definition of Imperialism provided by the SACP. Lenin talks about 'division' not 'integration'. Lenin argued that given inter-imperialist rivalries and contradictions, the big capitalist powers could not integrate. 'Integration' was not a feature or characteristic of the *stage* of Imperialism according to Lenin. For Lenin, there could not be such a 'notion' as 'Imperialist integration'. I had doubts about the Soviet position. I came to the conclusion that they subsumed a new development of capitalism, that is, capitalist economic integration under the banner of 'Imperialism' in a dogmatic way in order to argue that capitalism was still in the stage of Imperialism.

I decided to see if communist organizations had discussed capitalist economic integration. I went to the South African Communist Party (SACP) website and read an article on 'Globalization and the nation state' in 2001. One of its theses argued that 'Globalization' is the 'integration and marginalization of developing nations'… This was the closest I came to a discussion on 'integration' The SACP grounded 'Globalization' in Imperialism by arguing that 'Globalization is Imperialism'.

The problem with the position of the SACP, when they argue that Imperialism has the feature or characteristic of 'integration and marginalization of developing countries', is that it does not sit well with Lenin's definition of Imperialism provided by the SACP. In fact, the position of the SACP contradicts Lenin's position. Lenin does not talk about 'developing countries', 'integration', and 'marginalization' in his theory on the *stage* of Imperialism. I came to the conclusion that these new 'developments' were being subsumed under the banner of Imperialism, as the Soviets had done, without proper scientific analysis.

Two years later, in 2003, I was looking at the Communist Party of Britain website and came across a speech by its General Secretary on the 2003 Iraq War and capitalist globalization. He talks about 'integration' in relation to the European Union but comes to the conclusion that 'Globalization is Imperialism'. He discusses' integration' in a limited sense and subsumes it under the banner of Imperialism. I came to the general conclusion that for 'Marxism-Leninism' 'Globalization is Imperialism'.

'Integration' is a feature of 'Globalization' but not of Imperialism. The question arose: where to site 'capitalist economic integration' as it could not be sited within Lenin's theory of

Imperialism. I came to the slow realization that 'Globalization' and 'Imperialism' were two different stages of mature monopoly capitalism. This was the first part of my investigation.

The growing trend of capitalist economic integration and the concomitant political unity, for example, the G8 Summits, is a reflection of Lenin's understanding of Marx's two historical tendencies in the development of capitalism where he talks about the 'creation of the international unity of capital'. This has become a reality in the epoch of what Lenin called 'mature capitalism' with the development of the European Union, which is an economic union, premised on the full application of the General Law of Capitalist Accumulation. In his 2001 article on the National Question, published on its Website, Robert Griffiths, the General Secretary of the Communist Party of Britain (CPB) provides a 'textual' understanding of Marx's Remarks. Griffiths does not appear to be aware of Lenin's position on Marx's Remarks on the two tendencies in the historical development of capitalism and especially the 'creation of the international unity of capital' in order to further accumulation in the interest of the capitalists. It appears that the SACP leadership/theoreticians Nzimande and Cronin are blissfully ignorant of both Marx's position and the position of Lenin when they engage in 'sloganeering' that 'Globalization is Imperialism'. The essay on Globalization investigated capitalist economic integration and the concomitant political unity of the big capitalist powers as expressed in the G8 and G20 Summits on the basis of Lenin's concept 'the creation of the international unity of capital'.

The second part begins with researching 'Marx's concept of 'centralization'. This economic law, which has fascinated me since 1978 when I studied Marx's *Capital*, did not prevail in Lenin's time when he researched and wrote his work on Imperialism. Lenin based Imperialism on 'concentration' which I linked to Marx's General Law of Capitalist Accumulation. I discovered that Marx's concepts of 'the force of attraction' and 'the tendency to centralization' though takeovers, mergers and acquisitions prevailed in mature monopoly capitalism. The quote from Stelzer is the classical expression of Marx's concepts. He provides the validity of Marx's concepts in an unintentional way.

The problem arose of where to site 'centralization'. It could not be sited within Lenin's theory of Imperialism as he based it on 'concentration'. I came to the conclusion that 'centralization' had to be sited in 'Globalization' as it is a new development of 'mature monopoly capitalism'. It is from here onwards that I came to the slow realization that the *stage* of Globalization is underpinned by the four features of Marx's General Law of Capitalist Accumulation. Scientific Socialism, as developed by Marx, argues that 'mature monopoly capitalism' will express the workings of the General Law of Capitalist Accumulation. Marx is proved correct by these new developments of mature monopoly capitalism.

In 2011/12 I returned to my investigations. It dawned on me that capitalist economic integration leads to 'centralization' of the means of production and this was expressed by the development of the European Union. It was during this period that I realized that there were two sides to 'centralization' and this essay is an expression of that fact.

These 'two sides' of 'centralization' could not be sited in Lenin's theory of the *stage* of Imperialism which is premised on 'concentration of production and capital' and those features of economic and territorial *division* by the 'international trusts' and the big capitalist powers. I was 'forced' by the 'facts' to site centralisation in the *stage* of Globalization.

In 2013 there arose a debate on the 'working poor' and their conditions within mature monopoly capitalism. It proved the correctness of Marx's thesis of the deterioration in the condition of the working class in mature monopoly capitalism. This meant that there is the iron working-out of the 'absolute general law of capitalist accumulation'.

I did not start with the intention of proving Marx correct but my investigations and the facts, for example, the quote by Stelzer, led to these conclusions.

The investigations into the European Union which expresses both economic and political centralization led me to revisit Marx's main contradiction of capitalism that centralization of the means of production and the socialization of labour becomes incompatible with its capitalist integument. The European Union expresses such a contradiction as it embarks on the path of 'ever closer union'.

'Marxism-Leninism' is *silent* on a number of matters such as capitalist economic integration, 'centralization', on the full application of the General Law of Capitalist Accumulation, on the main contradiction of capitalism operating in the epoch of mature monopoly capitalism. 'Marxism-Leninism' cannot see these new developments because it sees mature monopoly capitalism through the 'absolute' prism of Imperialism and thus turns 'Leninism' into a dogma. Scientific Socialism argues that these new developments prevail in mature monopoly capitalism in the stage of Globalization.

I also discovered that the Treaty of Rome which consolidated the development towards capitalist economic integration on the continent of Europe is very much played down by 'Marxism-Leninism'. 'Marxism-Leninism' is blind or ignorant of the fact the big capitalist powers of Europe when they signed the Treaty of Rome decided to shed 'inter-imperialist rivalries' otherwise they could not co-operate in order to engage in economic integration, in the 'creation of the international unity of capital'. Furthermore, this was compounded by the termination of the system of Imperialist colonization due to the success of the national liberation revolutions and the existence, at that time, of 'World Socialism'. The Treaty of Rome signifies that the ruling class of the big capitalist powers in Europe decided to *unite* not only to preserve their economic power but also political power through the development of 'European 'democracy' from this time onwards and to 'suppress socialism' on the continent of Europe. Moreover, capitalist economic integration which the Treaty of Rome consolidated was in the interests of European finance capital and the big monopolies as it furthers 'capital accumulation'. The importance of the Treaty of Rome is that it signified the coming to the fore in the economic life of 'mature monopoly capitalism' of the second historical tendency of the 'universal law of capitalism' (Lenin) discovered by Marx which has led to capitalist economic integration in the form of the European Union, which is an economic union, resulting in the 'breakdown of national barriers' leading to the development of a European 'supra-national state' - notably a new development within 'mature monopoly capitalism'. The coming to the fore of the second historical tendency of the 'universal law of capitalism', signified through the Treaty of Rome is not an expression of Imperialism. Where to site it? This new development had to be sited within the stage of Globalisation, as one of its main features is capitalist economic integration. All the working class gets from 'Marxism-Leninism' is that this is 'Imperialism'. The European Union is viewed as an 'Imperialist bloc' by 'Marxism-Leninism'. The Treaty of Rome and the development of the European Union is a negation of this argument. The 28 nations of the European Union are not 'Imperialist powers'. Capitalist economic integration in Europe which has led to the formation of the European Union is a negation of what 'Marxism-Leninism' calls an 'imperialist bloc'. This puts to bed this dogma of 'Marxism-Leninism'.

The significance of the European Union within 'mature monopoly capitalism' in the stage of Globalization is that it negates the notion that the 'nation-state' is the 'absolute' form of capitalist development. This is a new development of mature monopoly capitalism which cannot be sited within the theory of Imperialism. It can only be sited in the *stage* of Globalization because this stage takes into account both European economic and political centralization ('supra-national' bodies) and national economic and political centralization in the form of the nation-state that arises through capitalist economic integration. Imperialism is not about the 'weakening and strengthening of the nation state' as the South African Communist Party argues. It is the stage of Globalization that is concerned with the changes that the' nation state' has undergone in the last twenty-five years. This is an important consequence of the Treaty of Rome which could not be sited within Lenin's theory of the stage of Imperialism.

The results of my investigations from all three essays led myself to contrast Scientific Socialism and 'Marxism-Leninism'. From the offset it was not my intention to do this. My intention simply was to ascertain the truth of the 'Marxist-Leninist' proposition 'Globalization is Imperialism'. The results of investigations proved the opposite, that 'Globalization is not Imperialism'.

The conclusion that Globalization is the new, higher and second stage of 'mature monopoly capitalism' was reached on the basis of the economic law, the General Law of Capitalist Accumulation, prevailing fully through its four features, with 'centralization' being the determining element.

In developing the working definition of the *stage* of Globalization, I tried to follow Marx's method in *Capital* 1. Marx did not explain fully the 'dialectic' of his work but he discussed his 'method' through the Russian reviewer of the *European Messenger* in the 'Afterword to the Second German Edition' in *Capital*. This is how the Russian reviewer discusses Marx's method. Marx begins the quote and then allows the Russian reviewer to describe his 'method':

After a quotation from the preface to my 'Criticism of Political Economy,' Berlin, 1859, pp. IV-VII, where I discuss the materialist basis of my method, the writer goes on: *"The one thing which is of moment to Marx, is to find the law of the phenomena with whose investigation he is concerned; and not only is that of moment to him, which governs these phenomena, in so far as they have a definite form and mutual connection within a given historical period. Of still greater moment to him is the law of their variation, of their development, I.e., of their transition from one form into another, from one series of connexions into a different one. This law once discovered, he investigates in detail the effects in which it manifests itself in social life. Consequently, Marx only troubles himself about one thing: to show, by rigid scientific investigation, the necessity of successive determinate orders of social conditions, and to establish, as impartially as possible, the facts that serve him for fundamental starting points. For this it is quite enough, if he proves, at the same time, both the necessity of the present order of things and the necessity of another order into which the first must inevitably pass over: and this is all the same, whether men believe or do not believe it, whether they are conscious or unconscious of it. Marx treats the social movement as a process of natural history, governed by laws not only independent of human will, consciousness and intelligence, but rather, on the contrary determining that will, consciousness and intelligence... If in the history of civilization, the conscious element plays a part so subordinate, then it is self-evident that a critical inquiry whose subject matter is civilization, can less than anything else, have for its basis any form of, or any result of, consciousness. That is to say, that not the idea but the material phenomenon alone can serve as its starting point. Such an inquiry will confine itself to the confrontation and the comparison of a fact, not with ideas, but with another fact. For this inquiry, the one thing of moment is, that both be investigated as accurately as possible and that they actually form, each with respect to the other, different momenta of an evolution; but most important of all is the rigid analysis of the series of successions, of the sequences and concatenations in which the different stages of such an evolution present themselves. But it will be said, the general laws of economic life are one and the same, no matter whether they are applied to the present and the past. This Marx directly denies. According to him, such abstract laws do not exist. On the contrary, in his opinion every historical period has laws of its own...As soon as society has outlived a given period of development and is passing over from given stage to another, it begins to be subject to other laws. In a word, economic life offers a phenomenon analogous to the history of evolution in other branches of biology. The old economists misunderstood the nature of economic laws when they likened them to the laws of physics and chemistry. A more thorough analysis of phenomena shows that social organisms differ among themselves as fundamentally as plants and animals. Nay, one and the same phenomenon falls under quite different laws in consequence of the different structure of those organisms as a whole, of the variations of their individual organs, of the different conditions in which these organs functions, &c. Marx, e.g., denies that the law of population is the same at all times and in all places. He asserts, on the contrary, that every stage of development has its own law of population... With the varying degree of development of productive power, social conditions and the laws governing them vary too. Whilst Marx sets himself the task of following and explaining from this point of view the economic system established by the sway of capital, he is only formulating, in strictly scientific manner, the aim that every accurate investigation into economic life must have. The scientific value of such an inquiry lies in the disclosing of the special laws that regulate the origin, existence, development, death of a given social organism and its replacement by another higher one. And it is this value that, in point of fact, Marx book has."*

This is what Marx says:

"Whilst the writer pictures what he takes to be actually my method, in this striking and [as far as concerns my own application of it] generous way, what else is he picturing but the dialectic method?"

I give this quote to the 'young' reader who comes to Scientific Socialism without any kind of assumptions so that he or she can come to an understanding of the 'dialectic method'.

I have given this quote about the 'dialectic method' of Marx because when I read the South African Communist Party (SACP) Political Report on their 'assumption' that 'Globalization is Imperialism' in 2001 I did so from this viewpoint. The SACP and its theoretician who wrote this Political Report, I assume it is Cronin, its Deputy General Secretary, even though it is presented by the General Secretary, Blade Nzimande, starts out from the premise 'Globalization is Imperialism' because Lenin's theory of Imperialism as the highest stage of capitalism is still relevant and they quote Lenin. Logically speaking, the 'Marxist-Leninist' SACP starts from simple identity, 'Globalization is Imperialism' which boils down to a tautology 'Imperialism is Imperialism' and then proceed to discuss the contradictions that arise in the 'historical period' or according to the SACP the 'new phase' of Imperialism known as 'Globalization' for example, 'weakens and strengthens the contemporary nation state'. This simple identity of 'Globalization is Imperialism' allows the SACP to take an 'anti-imperialist approach', to show their 'anti-imperialist credentials' against the approach of 'vulgar Marxism' and 'neo-liberalism'. This simple identity 'Globalization is Imperialism' has two sides: the first being the 'objective' which in this case is represented by Imperialism because 'capitalist globalization' is identified as Imperialism and the second is the 'subjective' which is to take an 'anti-imperialist approach'. On this basis, 'capitalist globalization' or 'globalization', the SACP 'believes' (SACP word), is a 'new phase' of Imperialism. By 'believing' it is a 'new phase' of Imperialism the SACP unintentionally declares that it is a 'historical period'. They refer to 'capitalist globalization' or 'globalization' as the 'quantitative and qualitative development and growth of Imperialism'. This 'historical period' or 'new phase' known as 'Globalization' is concerned with the 'quantitative and qualitative development and growth of Imperialism' and the contradictions that arise especially from the viewpoint of 'developing countries'.

The 'Marxist-Leninist' SACP sees itself as 'armed with theory', 'armed with dialectics'. It is important to look at its final thesis when it states 'Globalization simultaneously creates contradictions that lead to its own grave'. Given the SACP 'simple identity' that 'Globalization is Imperialism' this thesis should read: 'Imperialism simultaneously creates contradictions that lead to its own grave'. What contradictions Imperialism 'creates' is not known at present. Thus, the contradictions that the SACP discusses such as 'weakens and strengthens' and 'integration and marginalization' become the 'conditions of existence', together with new 'contradictions' 'created' which will lead Imperialism to its grave. The 'Marxist-Leninist' SACP 'theoretician/s' who constructed these theses fully understands that 'contradiction is the motive force of life' and base their theses on the dialectical law of contradiction. What is the 'main contradiction' among these 'contradictions' is not known? Is it Marx's main contradiction of capitalism or does it not apply in this 'historical period' known as 'Globalization' which the SACP 'designate' as a 'phase' of Imperialism?

The 'approach' of the SACP is based on the 'law of contradiction'. It is commendable. (In contrast, the Communist Party of Britain and their General Secretary, Rob Griffiths, do not show any understanding of 'dialectics'. The British Communists are not noted for their understanding of 'theory'.) In order to 'appreciate' this 'approach' it is important to remember that for the SACP 'globalization' refers to the 'quantitative and qualitative development and growth of Imperialism'. On this basis, the simple identity 'Globalization is Imperialism' is the first thesis and then the SACP develops theses that express the 'contradictions' which is a reflection of the 'quantitative and qualitative development and growth of Imperialism'. For the SACP these 'contradictions' represent the 'quantitative and qualitative development and growth of Imperialism' from the viewpoint of 'developing countries'. It is a one sided approach. The SACP 'talks' about the 'quantitative and qualitative development and growth of Imperialism' but fails to show the economic laws that have led to this situation, that has arisen in the 'historical period' 'Globalization' which they designate as the 'new phase of Imperialism' in its Theses. The second aspect that arises is put in a question: What is/are the 'qualitative development and growth'? This is not explained. The third aspect is put in a similar manner: What is/are the 'quantitative development and growth'? This is not explained. The SACP notion 'the quantitative and qualitative development and growth of Imperialism' is not quantified or qualified 'concretely' and thus becomes an 'abstract generality'. There are no 'concrete' facts to back up the proposition of the SACP that 'globalization' refers to the 'quantitative and qualitative development and growth of Imperialism'. The treatment of Lenin's concept 'Imperialism' by the SACP is to turn it, due to not being based on concrete facts, into an 'abstract generality' rather a 'concrete generality' which it was in Lenin's time. The 'law of contradiction' is not the appropriate 'law' to discuss Globalization, which the 'Marxist-Leninist' SACP theoreticians/leadership of Nzimande and Cronin describe as concerning capitalism and capital accumulation, and to the 'quantitative and qualitative development and growth of Imperialism'.

The reader is entitled to know what the SACP means by 'Globalization'. This is what the SACP states:

"Globalization is both an objective and subjective process. It is a logical development of a particular form of human practices – capitalism and capital accumulation."

Furthermore,

"Our starting point in understanding contemporary global realities should still be Lenin's analysis and understanding of Imperialism"

The SACP gives a couple of quotes from Lenin to justify their identity of 'Globalization' with Imperialism. From this 'assumption' (SACP word) the SACP comes to the conclusion:

"...what we refer to as globalization is a quantitative and qualitative development and growth of Imperialism."

The only logical conclusion to be reached, from the quotes given of the SACP position, in order to make it 'concrete,' is thus: 'globalization' is capitalism and capital accumulation; capitalism is Imperialism; globalization is 'referred' to as the 'quantitative and qualitative development and growth of Imperialism'.

It is one thing to identify 'Globalization' with Imperialism thus forming the thesis 'Globalization is Imperialism'. It is another thing to identify 'Globalization' as the 'quantitative and qualitative development and growth of Imperialism'. In using the quotes from the SACP 'the quantitative and qualitative development and growth of Imperialism' can only refer to the 'quantitative and qualitative development and growth of capital accumulation' because 'globalization', according to the SACP, is both capitalism and capital accumulation and Imperialism. This is the only way to make sense of this phrase 'quantitative and qualitative development and growth'... Yet, there is an *absence* of discussion on 'globalization' as 'capital accumulation. There is a sore lack of economic facts and economic laws to explain the 'quantitative and qualitative development and growth of Imperialism' as a representation of 'capitalist accumulation'. It shows that there is lacking the application of *materialist* dialectics. There are no economic facts or laws to back the thesis 'Globalization is Imperialism'. It has to be pointed out to the SACP that Rob Griffiths grounds 'globalization' in 'concentration of economic resources...' At least, Griffiths starts out on materialist premise whereas the SACP does not. The 'Marxist-Leninist' SACP also fails to show which economic laws that are responsible for the contradictions of Globalization (read as Imperialism). The dialectical law of contradiction is not the appropriate law to reflect their assertion 'Globalization is Imperialism' which is concerned with 'capital accumulation'.

From the first thesis, 'Globalization is Imperialism' there is a 'leap' to its second thesis, 'Globalization is the simultaneous integration and marginalization of developing countries'. The SACP does not show the 'moments' and mediations' through economic facts and economic laws from its first thesis that lead to the development of this 'contradiction' in its second thesis. In contrast, Marx shows the economic law, the 'moments' and 'mediations' that lead to him developing the 'main contradiction of capitalism': that centralization of the means of production and the socialization of labour become incompatible with its capitalist integument.

In order to understand the 'logic' of the SACP it is important to 'understand' Lenin's 'law of uneven development'. Lenin argued that 'mature capitalism' which he called Imperialism or 'mature monopoly capitalism' (Griffith's words) would be characterized by the law of uneven development. In the 'historical period' known as 'Globalization' (At this 'juncture' the concern is not whether it is a stage or a phase) this law shows itself in the relationship between what the SACP calls 'developing countries' or as bourgeois ideologists call 'emerging countries' and other categories, and the 'advanced capitalist countries'. This law is expressed in the contradiction 'integration and marginalization of developing countries'. Furthermore, The SACP states that 'Globalization' is 'capitalism and capital accumulation'. It follows that the General Law of Capitalist Accumulation prevails and shows itself in the contradiction 'integration and marginalization of developing countries' because 'capital accumulation' is in the favour of the 'advanced capitalist countries'. Thus, there are two 'materialist laws' that show themselves in the contradiction. It is only then that the contradiction can be fully regarded as expressing 'objective reality'. This 'approach' tries to follow the 'method' of Marx. The SACP does not engage in the expression of its theses through Marx's 'method' but in 'abstract generality' known as 'the quantitative and qualitative development and growth of Imperialism'. It is clear that for the SACP, 'the quantitative and qualitative development and growth of Imperialism' has led to the development of the contradiction 'integration and marginalization of developing countries' in this 'historical period known as 'Globalization'.

The SACP makes the 'assumption' that 'Globalization is Imperialism'. The SACP provides quotes from Lenin, one of which is a definition of Imperialism, because this is their 'starting-point' as the SACP argues that Lenin's theory of Imperialism is still relevant to analyze 'contemporary global realities'.

One of the features of this 'definition' by Lenin provided by the SACP is this:

"…in which the division of the world among the international trusts has begun…"

For the SACP 'globalization' is an expression of this feature of the definition of Imperialism by Lenin because of their 'assumption' that 'Globalization is Imperialism'. This 'assumption' that 'Globalization is Imperialism' expressing this feature of 'division' is negated and contradicted by the Communist Party of Britain's (CPB) statement at its 52nd Congress that the 'EU is a creation of Western Europe big monopolies and is designed to serve their interests'. It is clear from the CPB statement that the 'big monopolies' of Western Europe have created the EU (European Union) which is an economic union, which is a form of capitalist economic integration. The only logical and realistic conclusion to be reached is that 'big monopolies' of Western Europe by creating the EU are engaged in 'integration'. This 'fact' contradicts not only this feature of Imperialism but it contradicts the SACP own 'assumption' that 'Globalization is Imperialism'. It is the CPB that disproves both Lenin and the SACP 'assumption' that 'Globalization is Imperialism'.

Furthermore, the SACP contradiction of 'integration and marginalization of developing countries' disproves Lenin's features of economic and territorial *division* by the 'international trusts' and the big capitalist powers in the latter definition of the stage of Imperialism. 'Integration' and 'marginalization' are not identical or can be identified with 'division'. The SACP is oblivious to this 'contradiction' in its 'logical' presentation through its first two theses.

It is the 'starting-point' (SACP word) or 'beginning' that causes a major problem. Given that 'globalization' referred to as 'the quantitative and qualitative development and growth of Imperialism' (which is an 'abstract' statement and not 'concrete' expressing economic facts and economic laws,) because Lenin's theory of Imperialism is still relevant, the SACP *decrees* that 'Globalization is Imperialism' which leads the SACP into dogmatism. It fails to explain through economic facts and 'laws' *why* Lenin's theory is still relevant to analyze 'contemporary global realities'. It fails to explain what changes state monopoly capitalism has gone through in the 'historical period' known as 'Globalisation' and what laws have arisen that have caused these changes. The SACP does not look at the social phenomenon as Marx advised by analyzing 'globalization' in-itself and for-itself in order to ascertain whether Globalization is a stage or a phase of Imperialism. What it does is to 'decree' 'Globalization is Imperialism'. The SACP *objective* is to 'decree' that Lenin's theory of the stage of Imperialism is still relevant to 'defining' what 'globalization' is. Thus, the SACP sinks into *subjectivism* because it does not apply the 'method' of Marx. The 'starting-point' is not based on Lenin's dictum 'concrete analysis of a concrete situation'.

The SACP states:

"As the SACP has consistently said, to engage with global realities without a sufficient analysis of its capitalist character is bound to lead to a lot of problems."

What the SACP does when it refers 'globalization' as 'the quantitative and qualitative development of growth of Imperialism' is to use logical categories for example, 'quantitative', qualitative', rather than provide 'a sufficient analysis of its capitalist character' which leads to problems.

The SACP, in 'beginning' its thesis 'Globalization is Imperialism' by referring to 'globalization' as 'the quantitative and qualitative development and growth of Imperialism' is engaged in the 'movement of logical categories', for example, 'quantitative', qualitative', rather than the 'movement of economic facts' or 'economic laws'. This is the weakness of its 'dialectics'.

I would like to repeat a quote that I gave in the main body so as to illustrate the difference between Marx's 'dialectic method' and the 'approach' of the SACP' more concretely. The SACP has this to say on the 'term' 'globalization':

"But when we speak of globalization as being essentially a new phase of Imperialism, we are reminding ourselves that it is a process that is riven with systemic contradictions, that is based on super-exploitation, and that is simultaneously a process of development and systematic under-development."

The SACP argues that 'Globalization' is 'a new phase of Imperialism'. There are no economic laws to support this assertion. All we have is the SACP 'ideas' of 'systemic contradictions', 'super-exploitation', 'development' and 'systematic under-development' under-pinning this 'historical period' or 'phase'.

Marx, when he discussed the main contradiction of capitalism: that centralization of the means of production and the socialization of labour become incompatible with its capitalist integument based this 'contradiction' on the particular law of centralization derived from the General Law of Capitalist Accumulation. The SACP talks about 'systemic contradictions' (which is the main one we do not know) but there is no under-pinning with economic law/s. It is 'phrase-mongering' not materialist dialectics. Scientific Socialism raises the question to the 'Marxist-Leninist' SACP: What are the economic law/s underpinning 'systemic contradictions' of the 'historical period' which they call 'Globalization' as the 'new phase of Imperialism'. What are the economic laws underpinning the 'quantitative and qualitative development and growth of Imperialism'? The SACP is 'silent' on these questions or it has not addressed it.

It is clear that the 'approach' of the SACP, in terms of 'methodology' is far away from that of Marx's 'dialectic method'. They have not discussed the 'law' or 'laws' governing the 'phenomenon' 'Globalization' which they 'term' as the 'new phase of Imperialism.' When Marx investigated and analyzed 'capitalist accumulation', he did so through the General Law of Capitalist Accumulation though its four 'particularities': concentration, centralization, organic composition of capital and the industrial reserve army. He then develops the main contradiction of capitalism which is derived from the General Law of Capitalist Accumulation though one of its 'particularities', that of 'centralization'.

Their approach also differs from Lenin. Lenin, when he investigated 'Imperialism' based it on the 'particular' economic law 'concentration'. He then proceeds to discuss the features or characteristics of Imperialism. For Lenin, Imperialism was the 'form' or 'superstructure' (Lenin's concept) of 'state monopoly capitalism'. His 'approach' follows that of Marx. The SACP 'approach', through its theses, is not based on any economic law and this differentiates it from the method of Marx and Lenin. The SACP 'approach' is more akin to Hegelian dialectics. It is, as I have pointed out already, begins with 'simple identity' which is an 'abstract generality' that expresses 'contradictions' and these 'contradictions' will lead to the demise of the 'phenomenon' under discussion.

Marx not only developed 'dialectics' by developing *materialist* dialectics, he also developed *'historical* materialism'. The analysis of Imperialism by the SACP because it identifies 'globalization' as Imperialism must be on the basis of 'historical materialism' and specifically by 'political economy' which must take into account laws that govern economic behavior. In the SACP case concerning 'Globalization' (read as Imperialism) there are no economic law or laws 'determining' the contradiction 'integration and marginalization of developing countries', for example. It is true, as the SACP shows, that the 'advanced capitalist countries' want 'developing countries' to 'open up' their economies for exploitation, to use the SACP words, 'super-exploitation' leading to 'development and systematic underdevelopment'. The 'advanced capitalist countries', at the behest of their finance capitalists and monopoly capitalists, want, what the intelligent bourgeois ideologists call, 'financial liberalization' so as to further and raise 'capital accumulation'. The policy of the 'advanced capitalist countries' in the 'historical period' known as 'Globalization' is 'financial liberalization' as concerning 'developing countries' or according to bourgeois ideologists 'emerging countries'. What law or laws is this based on? The SACP is 'silent'. This is why I have said that it is a one-sided approach based on a 'partisanship' of taking an 'anti-imperialist approach' from the standpoint of 'developing countries' especially the continent of Africa. This does not explain the 'quantitative and qualitative development and growth of Imperialism' as the SACP claims 'Globalization' is. *Materialist* dialectics and *'historical* materialism' demands that a law-governed and comprehensive approach be taken when analyzing social phenomenon such as 'Globalization' and not be one-sided as the SACP is guilty of. 'Historical materialism' demands that laws of the social phenomenon within a 'historical period' under investigation be discovered and show how they apply in social life and the contradictions that arise. The SACP 'approach', in presenting its theses, is one-sided in that it only shows what it regards as the 'contradictions' of Imperialism or 'Globalization' because of its assertion 'Globalization is Imperialism'.

It 'becomes' clear that all the SACP does in these theses is to shout 'Globalization is

Imperialism', show the 'contradictions' that have developed and this from the standpoint of 'developing countries' in order to take an 'anti-imperialist approach'. It is a crass 'approach' that does not provide 'a sufficient analysis' of the 'capitalist character' of 'Globalization' given that it is 'capital accumulation' as the SACP states. This leads to 'problems' for the SACP especially in relation to its first thesis.

I also looked at the 2003 speech of Rob Griffiths, the General Secretary of the Communist Party of Britain (CPB) from the same viewpoint. He, also, starts from the premise 'Globalization is Imperialism' and argues that it is the 'third phase' of Imperialism having underpinning this 'historical period' on 'concentration of economic resources…' Griffiths slavishly and dogmatically follows Lenin in this sense. By arguing thus, he blinkered himself to other laws applying during this 'historical period'. He fails to see that 'centralization' prevails in the epoch of mature monopoly capitalism, in the 'historical period' known as 'Globalization'. So does the 'organic composition of capital' in both the *technical* and *value* sense, and also the 'industrial reserve army'. Marx's economic law, the General Law of Capitalist Accumulation prevails fully in the epoch of mature monopoly capitalism which is in the stage of Globalization. Scientific Socialism argues that given the present 'historical period', which is known as the stage of Globalization, it is underpinned by the General Law of Capitalist Accumulation. Monopoly capitalism in the twenty first century cannot be based solely on 'concentration' as Griffiths does. Griffiths 'absolutizes' 'concentration' and thus fails to see the relationship between the 'general' and the 'particular' given a 'historical period'. This is due to being a dogmatist. It appears that Griffiths is unaware of, is blind to or is simply ignorant of Marx's General Law of Capitalist Accumulation.

It is important to understand the 'Marxist-Leninist' 'world-view' based on Imperialism. It is shaped by Lenin's proposition that 'Imperialism is the highest stage of capitalism'. For 'Marxism-Leninism' there can be no other stage. 'Marxism-Leninism' holds fast to this 'absolute' of Lenin. It is not I that proves Lenin's theory of Imperialism out-moded and outdated. First and foremost, it is the changes in mature monopoly capitalism that have *negated* Lenin's theory of the stage of Imperialism, for example, capitalist economic integration. Secondly, it is the 'Marxist-Leninist' organizations like the SACP and the CPB, who in maintaining 'Globalization is Imperialism', and thus dogmatically defending the notion that capitalism is still in the stage of Imperialism, *contradict* Lenin's definition of the *stage* of Imperialism. The 'absolute' of Lenin that 'Imperialism is the highest stage of capitalism' cannot be held. By holding fast to this 'absolute', 'Marxism-Leninism' as an 'ideology' of the working class, and 'Marxist-Leninist' organizations like the CPB, have shown themselves to be 'blinkered' to new developments of mature monopoly capitalism. The 'prism' of Imperialism which 'Marxism-Leninism' views the capitalist world with gives it a myopic worldview. In the process, 'Marxism-Leninism' treats Marx as a 'dead-dog'. Marx's remarks on 'mature monopoly capitalism' as described by the General Secretary of the Communist Party of Britain are ignored. Also ignored is Lenin's understanding of Marx's remarks on the two tendencies in the historical development of capitalism. This was one of the results of my investigation. 'Marxism-Leninism', by its dogmatic assertion that 'Globalization is Imperialism', does not provide an *objective* analysis of mature monopoly capitalism in the present 'historical period', but sinks into *subjectivism* entailing a 'gut-hatred' of capitalism and Imperialism. This is clear in the case of the individual examples, Rob Griffiths, the General Secretary of the Communist Party of Britain and the SACP and its theoretician/s.

In the case of the General Secretary of the Communist Party of Britain, Rob Griffiths, his analysis that 'Globalization is Imperialism', the 'third phase' of Imperialism, lacks credibility because the CPB position is that 'Globalization' is a 'term' and lacks 'class essence'. Therefore, how does he conclude that 'Globalization' is the 'third phase' of Imperialism is a 'mystery' to Scientific Socialism? What makes 'Globalization' a 'term' and not a 'scientific concept' is not explained by both the SACP and the CPB. What makes 'Globalization' a 'phase' of Imperialism is not explained scientifically. Both 'Marxist-Leninist' parties have not applied the 'method' of Marx, the 'dialectic method' in their assertion that 'Globalization is Imperialism'.

It, thus, becomes clear that 'Marxism-Leninism' by asserting that 'Globalization is Imperialism' is a 'subjectivist' and 'emotive', in a word, are demonstrating a 'gut-reaction' to bourgeois ideologists who crowed that capitalism is in the stage of Globalization.

What 'Marxism-Leninism' did, from my investigations, was to analyze the 'arguments' of bourgeois ideologists who maintained that capitalism had changed and was in the stage of Globalization. From my investigations of the works of bourgeois ideologists on 'Globalization' I came to the conclusion that they had to be rejected because their analyses based on bourgeois economics and economic history did not make sense. In this sense, I came to similar conclusions as 'Marxism-Leninism'. However, I did not designate 'Globalization' as a 'term' which lacks 'class essence' as the CPB does. I investigated 'Globalization' from the viewpoint of Scientific Socialism and came to certain conclusions.

Scientific Socialism uses the 'dialectic method' of Marx to analyze the economic life of mature monopoly capital by stating that it is in the stage of Globalization because the General Law of Capitalist Accumulation fully prevails and rejects the dogmatism of 'Marxism-Leninism' that 'Globalization is Imperialism'.

I say that the closest I came to, in my investigations, of a communist organization asserting that monopoly capital is in the stage of Globalization was from the website of the Communist Party of the United States of America (CPUSA). In a report 'Labor in the Era of Capitalist Globalization' (From teleconference on labor unity, June 9, 2005) there was this statement:

"Lenin made it clear in his Imperialism: The Highest Stage of Capitalism, that Imperialism is not a policy. It is a stage of capitalist development, an objective process. The same is true of capitalist globalization. It is not a policy of this or that government. It is an objective process of transnational capitalist development. This distinction is important to understanding the class struggle today..."

Let us be clear in the analysis of this statement. The first thing to note is that it is talking about 'capitalist globalization'. The second point to note is that this statement argues that Imperialism was a stage of capitalist development and on this basis argues that the same is true of capitalist globalization. 'Capitalist globalization' is a stage of capitalism. The third point to note is that is that this statement grounds the stage of 'capitalist globalization' in 'objective process of transnational capitalist development'.

Scientific Socialism agrees with the above statement that 'Globalization' is a stage of mature monopoly capitalist development. Scientific Socialism, however, differs from this statement in one respect. Scientific Socialism grounds 'Globalization' in Marx's General Law of Capitalist Accumulation. It is clear that 'transnational capitalist development' is not an economic law. The above statement does not ground 'capitalist globalization' under any economic law or laws. This is the 'problematic' of the above-statement. The objective growth of 'transnational' monopolies must be looked at from the viewpoint of Marx's economic concept of 'centralization' and not simply on 'concentration'.

Scientific Socialism, in grounding 'Globalization' in the General Law of Capitalist Accumulation, presents an important understanding of the class struggle today.

The more monopoly capitalism develops in its mature epoch; it leads to new economic laws coming to the fore. Communists, thus, have to explain scientifically how these new economic laws effect social life, especially the class struggle. For example, Marx argued that in 'mature monopoly capitalism' there would be the 'iron' working of the 'absolute general law of capitalist accumulation'. Nowhere is this clearer than in Britain It manifests itself in the words of the British Prime Minister, Cameron, the 'working poor'. The deterioration in the lot of the working class in Britain is becoming starker every day. During the era of 'New Labour' in Britain from 1997 to 2010, the rich got richer and the poor poorer, the capitalist class got richer and the working class poorer reflects the working of the absolute general law of capitalist accumulation. The conclusion is that the capitalist mode of production, capitalism, only works in the interests of capitalist class not in the interests of the working class in Britain. Britain in 2014 is in the stage of recovery within the capitalist economic cycle. The British coalition government of Conservatives and Liberal Democrats is trying to convince the British working class that the capitalist 'recovery' is in the interests of the working class. It is clear that the rise in capitalist accumulation in the 'recovery' stage is only in the interests of the capitalist class not the working class and the latter is becoming aware of it. For Scientific Socialism this 'state of affairs' leads to Marx's main contradiction that the centralization of the means of production and the socialization of labour becomes incompatible with its capitalist integument. The British Communists, for example, the 'Marxist-Leninist' Communist Party of Britain and the New Communist Party, who view British monopoly capitalism through the prism of Imperialism, fail to explain these developments scientifically to its working class especially its 'advanced workers' (Lenin).

'Marxism-Leninism', from the days of Soviet socialism to the present day, fails to scientifically analyze the Treaty of Rome which has led to the development of the European Union. It is clear that the Treaty of Rome, which signified the development of capitalist economic integration, at first with the European Economic Community (EEC) as a customs union, and secondly with the European Union as an economic union, has underpinning it the second historical tendency of the 'universal law of capitalism' discovered by Marx and discussed by Lenin and the General Law of Capitalist Accumulation especially centralization. This is the position of Scientific Socialism which base its analysis of the Treaty of Rome on the laws that Marx discovered.

I started out with investigating the propositional statement 'Globalization is Imperialism'. In the process of investigation there arose a contrast between Scientific Socialism and 'Marxism-Leninism'. I had to subordinate my personal views and ideas in order to present the contrasting positions that arose from the investigations. These essays are an expression of the difficulties faced.

As I investigated the propositional statement 'Globalization is Imperialism' I became disappointed with the South African Communist Party, (which I respected as a revolutionary party), position on Globalization because it was not grounded in any economic law. I realized that its Theses on 'Globalization is Imperialism' were not based on the dialectic method of Marx. In the recent period (2012-2014) I became aware that some of its theses contradict Lenin's definition of Imperialism which they provided in their Report. As I have shown 'integration', 'marginalization', 'developing countries', are not features of the *stage* of Imperialism as defined by Lenin which they provide but were features of modern 'mature monopoly capitalism'. I, objectively, had to include it in the working definition of Globalization that was constructed and provided by myself.

It was the SACP 'beginning', its 'starting-point', its first thesis that 'Globalization is Imperialism' that caused the greatest difficulty and problem. I have tried to examine it in relation to my understanding of Marx's 'dialectic method'. I found the SACP 'wanting' in this respect both in terms of 'philosophically' and its 'absence' of 'economics' of 'Globalization'.

As for the 'Marxist-Leninist' South African Communist Party (SACP) position on socialism through the South African Road to Socialism I was confronted between its statement that socialism is a transitional social system between capitalism and communism with a mixed economy and Marx and Lenin's position that the co-operative system is the system of socialism. Furthermore, the SACP advocates 'public' or 'state ownership' and the 'strengthening' of the National Democratic State in the second phase of the National Democratic Revolution (NDR). It became obvious to me that 'Marxism-Leninism' has a 'fetish' for 'public ownership' as is the case with the Communist Party of Britain (CPB) which states that it 'public ownership' is the 'essence of socialism'.

I turn to the Communist Party of Britain. I am very mindful of Engels statement that the British lack theory. The CPB's position is the same as the SACP which is 'Globalization is Imperialism'. Both view Globalization as a 'term' and as a 'phase' of Imperialism. The difference between the two was that the General Secretary of the CPB Rob Griffiths grounds Globalization in the particular economic law 'concentration', following Lenin, and that it lacks 'class essence'. I became aware of the dogmatism of the 'Marxist-Leninist' CPB. Its lack of theory shows when it is blind to and ignorant of Marx's very important concept and economic law, that of 'centralization'. The General Secretary of the CPB, Rob Griffiths shows his dogmatism when he clings so rigidly to the 'particular' economic law 'concentration' but is ignorant of the 'general' economic law, Marx's General Law of Capitalist Accumulation. In the epoch of modern mature monopoly capitalism, which Scientific Socialism states is in the stage of Globalization based on the General Law of Capitalist Accumulation fully prevailing through its four features, concentration, centralization, the organic composition of capital and the industrial reserve army, the 'Marxist-Leninist' Rob Griffiths and the CPB cannot cite 'concentration', as the sole determinant of state monopoly capitalism in the twenty first century as Lenin was able to do nearly a hundred years ago (I have already explained this position between the 'general' and the 'particular' above).

There was the statement by the CPB on the EU being a creation of Western Europe big monopolies in its Congress documents. It took me a while to appreciate the significance of the CPB statement. It dawned on me that the CPB statement contradicted and disproved Lenin's argument that the monopolies are engaged in economic partitioning or division of the world. It also became clear to me that the SACP theses, for example, on the 'weakening and strengthening of the nation state' and 'integration and marginalization of developing countries' and the CPB statement on the EU contradicted Lenin's definition of the stage of Imperialism provided by the SACP. They cannot be subsumed under the banner of Imperialism. The development of the European Union has led to the 'weakening of the nation state' and has affected 'national sovereignty. In Britain, the Conservative Party Members of Parliament are always talking about how the EU is affecting 'national sovereignty' and the British nation state. The 'weakening' of the nation state and the effect on 'national sovereignty' within the European Union is not due to inter-imperialist rivalry and contradictions but is due to capitalist economic integration in the form of an economic union. I could not ground this fact in the definition of Imperialism by Lenin provided by the SACP. This is a new development of mature monopoly capitalism that could only be grounded in the working definition of the stage of Globalization provided by myself.

It was these 'inconsistencies' by both the CPB and the SACP and by 'Marxism-Leninism' in general that 'forced' me to change my 'bedrock' view that Imperialism is the highest stage of capitalism. There arose a contrast between the positions of Scientific Socialism and 'Marxism-Leninism'. Furthermore, this was made more complicated because there is difference between Marx and Lenin on the economic law which develops monopoly capital. Engels points out, in his editing of Capital, Vol. 1, that 'centralization' is linked to 'monopoly'. Lenin cites 'concentration' as the economic law that 'created' monopoly capital or monopolies. Lenin proved Marx's economic law 'concentration'. Stelzer proved Marx's economic law 'centralization' and the economic concept 'force of attraction'. This led me to the conclusion that Marx's General Law of Capitalist Accumulation fully prevailed in mature monopoly capitalism. It also led me to the conclusion that Globalization, a 'historical period', is the new higher stage of mature monopoly capitalism. It was the results of my investigation into such matters that led me to consider that Scientific Socialism is the scientific ideology of the working class not 'Marxism-Leninism'.

This became very clear with the CPB statement that 'public ownership...is the essence of socialism'. I could not trace its roots in the works of Marx and Lenin. Instead, I found that 'Marxism-Leninism' does not adhere to Marx and Lenin's position that the co-operative system is the system of socialism. I know that the 'Marxist-Leninist' Rob Griffiths has read Lenin's article 'On Co-operation'. He stated this in one of his speeches published on the CPB website. He does not fully understand the significance of Lenin's statement that 'the system of civilized co-operators is the system of socialism.' My investigation led to the conclusion the position of the CPB and that of Lenin is diametrically opposed. Where are the 'roots' of the CPB position to be found? I could only trace it to 'Stalinism' which espouses 'state ownership' or 'public ownership'. The furthest that I could go back to was War Communism which Lenin called 'state monopoly' and he rejected it.

The most difficult to write but the easiest to get to grips with was the 'philosophy of socialist humanity'. Given the results of my investigations into the 'state monopoly' system and its consequences, I researched the co-operative movement within capitalism. The ethos of 'co-operation' had to be applied to the socialist mode of production which for Lenin is the 'system of civilized co-operators' if a 'philosophy of socialist humanity' is to be feasible. I give the basic rudiments from the results of my investigation starting from the economic base, the co-operative system, so that there can be widespread discussion.

I was most struck by the lack of understanding of *materialist* dialectics as developed by Karl Marx by the leaders of the 'Marxist-Leninist' organizations discussed. The 'approach' of the General Secretary of the Communist Party of Britain, Rob Griffiths and his organization is eclectic especially his 2003 speech. The 'approach' of the South African Communist Party Theses on Globalization is bereft of *materialist* dialectics. Both have one thing in common. They both subsume new developments of mature monopoly capitalism under the banner of Imperialism. This is not the scientific approach of *materialist* dialectics.

I have given the results of my investigations to the world and to the working class in particular, especially the 'advanced workers' who are thirsty for knowledge concerning modern mature monopoly capitalism. At the beginning of the essay on the Soviet 'model' or 'system' of socialism, I gave a quote by Marx on the proletarian revolutions of the 19th century. These essays are a 'criticism' of the present 'state' of 'Marxism-Leninism' and its organizations that adhere to this ideology even though I did not set out with this intention. I had to tear asunder that 'coziness' that 'Marxism-Leninism' provides for communists who view mature monopoly capitalism through the prism of Imperialism and the system of socialism based on 'public ownership' or 'state ownership'. Due to the results of the investigations concerned, I was forced to engage in this task. It was not of my choosing.

For myself, these essays allowed me to 're-engage' with Scientific Socialism and the principles developed by Marx, Engels and Lenin.

I would like to say that these essays were not intended, in the first place, to be 'polemical'. It was through the investigations into Marx's General Law of Capitalist Accumulation and the growing trend of capitalist economic integration especially the European Union that forced myself to be 'critical' of the positions of the South African Communist Party and the Communist Party of Britain and 'Marxism-Leninism' in general.

The SACP views that monopoly capitalism is still in the stage of Imperialism, 'decrees' that 'Globalization is Imperialism', justified by quotes from Lenin, then proceeds to discuss the 'contradictions', especially from the viewpoint of 'developing countries', leading to the demise of Imperialism. This 'approach' ignored the changes that monopoly capitalism has undergone in the 'historical period' known as 'Globalization' or 'capitalist globalization' especially in the 'advanced capitalist countries' where monopoly capital and finance capital is dominant. The SACP is 'silent' on 'this side' in the presentation of its Theses. For the SACP, given that 'Globalization is Imperialism', the 'North' (SACP word) is responsible for the 'development and under-development' of 'developing countries' and thus an 'anti-imperialist approach' must be taken. It is this 'partisanship' that shapes its Theses and does not allow it to present a 'comprehensive' analysis of 'Globalization', of looking at 'developments' in the 'North' as well.

The investigations that I conducted 'forced' me to look at both finance-capital and the monopolies in the 'advanced capitalist countries' and the policy of 'financial liberalization' (bourgeois ideologists notion which I have maintained) that they imposed on 'developing countries' in the' historical period' known as 'Globalization'. The working definition of the *stage* of 'Globalization' that has been constructed takes both into account.

The SACP talks about '... massive changes that have taken place...' It became clear that finance capital and the monopolies in the 'advanced capitalist countries' had undergone 'massive changes' during the 'historical period' known as 'Globalization'. This was evident in the 'development and growth' (SACP words) of 'takeovers, mergers and acquisitions' in the 'advanced capitalist countries'. Went, a student of the Trotskyite Mandel, in his analysis of 'Globalization' shows this 'development and growth'. The only problem with the analysis of 'Globalization' by Went is that there is no 'connection' with the economic laws of capitalism discovered by Karl Marx.

'Marxism-Leninism' in general, and the SACP and the CPB, as individual organizations, does not discuss this 'development and growth' within 'mature monopoly capitalism'. It was when I came across Stelzer's article that I became convinced that 'takeovers, mergers and acquisitions' were expressions of 'force of attraction' and 'the tendency to centralization'. The 'principles' and methodology of Scientific Socialism dictated and determined that I had to make the 'connection' between 'takeovers, mergers and acquisitions' and 'centralization'. This 'development and growth' of 'centralization' within 'mature monopoly capitalism' in the 'historical period' known as 'Globalization' *negates* the SACP 'assumption' that 'Globalization' is the 'quantitative and qualitative development and growth of Imperialism'.

It is clear that Marx's General Law of Capitalist Accumulation, through its four particularities: concentration, centralization, the organic composition of capital and the industrial reserve army, prevails in the economic life of 'mature monopoly capitalism' in the second decade of the twenty first century. Communists must come to this 'understanding' and develop revolutionary theory in accordance with this 'change'. The working definition of the stage of Globalization provides a guide as to how revolutionary theory has to be developed. Foremost, given this working definition, is the 'deterioration in the lot of the working class'. Poverty, which expresses Marx concept, is rife both in the 'advanced capitalist countries' and the 'developing countries'. Capitalism cannot meet the needs and wants of the working class and the industrial reserve army. The General Law of Capitalist Accumulation application in economic life of 'mature monopoly capitalism' shows clearly the 'super-exploitation' (SACP word) that finance-capital and the monopolies are engaged with.

Finally, given these 'changes' in 'mature monopoly capitalism' that I discovered in my investigations the biggest problem faced was where to 'site' these 'changes'. These 'changes' could not be expressed through Lenin's theory of Imperialism. The 'growing trend of capitalist economic integration' is the direct opposite, nay, contradiction of Lenin's position of the economic 'division' by the international trusts and the territorial division of the world by the big capitalist powers. Finance-capital and the monopolies, for example, within the European Union, are engaged in capitalist economic 'integration' through an economic union and it is this fact that contradicts Lenin's position.

Furthermore, US finance-capital and monopolies, represented by the Obama Administration, is engaged in negotiations to form 'free-trade areas' both with the European Union and in the Pacific region in 2014. A 'free-trade area' is a form of capitalist economic integration. US finance-capital and monopolies are using this form of capitalist economic integration to raise and further 'capital accumulation' in its interests and its 'image'. Why is the United States of America finance capital and monopolies so 'engaged' (SACP word) in a 'free-trade area' (FTA)? It is because this form of 'capitalist economic integration' does not involve 'weakening of the nation state' nor affect 'national sovereignty' according to Professor Nevin, in his work, *The Economics of Europe*.

In the beginning of the essay on 'Globalization', I gave Rob Griffiths, the General Secretary of the Communist Party of Britain, 'understanding' of Marx's *Remarks on the National Question* and the 'two conflicting tendencies in the development of capitalism'. I am concerned with the second 'tendency' which is that 'capitalism tends to breakdown national barriers as trade, economic life generally, politics and culture become more 'international''. Finance capital and the monopolies, in the epoch of 'mature monopoly capitalism', is for the 'breakdown [of] national barriers' as this furthers 'capital accumulation'. The European Union is a concrete expression of the 'breakdown [of] national barriers' in order to further 'capital accumulation' and proves the correctness of Marx's propositions on developments in 'mature monopoly capitalism'. I had to work out the 'roots' of this development and my investigation showed that it had to be 'rooted' in the Treaty of Rome where it first came to the fore.

The SACP, by making the 'assumption' that 'Globalization is Imperialism', through referring 'Globalization' as the 'quantitative and qualitative development and growth of Imperialism', which enables it to take an 'anti-imperialist approach' from the viewpoint of 'developing countries', fails to take into account this 'second tendency' in the development of capitalism that Marx remarked on, and described by Rob Griffiths, in its Theses. The SACP takes a myopic view of 'Globalization', which expresses this 'second tendency', because of taking an 'anti-imperialist approach', of identifying 'Globalization' as Imperialism and from the viewpoint of 'developing countries'. In this sense, the SACP treats Marx as a 'dead-dog'. It is also a 'one-sided approach'. The SACP sees itself as a 'Marxist-Leninist' organization. It only sees 'Leninism' and patently fails to see, in constructing its Theses, Marx's remarks on 'mature capitalism', on the 'universal law of capitalism' (Lenin) or what Lenin called 'revolutionary Marxism'. This is because the SACP 'starting-point' or 'entry-point' is Lenin's analysis of capitalism in the stage of Imperialism. That is why it can only express its Theses in terms of 'contradictions' of Imperialism given that the SACP claims that 'Globalization is Imperialism'. It is ignorant of Marx's 'dialectic method' and the 'two conflicting tendencies in the development of capitalism' as described by the General Secretary of the Communist Party of Britain, Rob Griffiths.

The SACP 'argues' that these Theses 'might' not be about 'Globalization *per se*' but it could be about 'Globalization and the nation state'. It is not about 'Globalization'. Its Theses, once it has shouted 'Globalization is Imperialism', is to show the 'super-exploitation' of 'developing countries' and the effect on the nation state in those countries. It does not look at the 'advanced capitalist countries' and how their 'nation- state' is affected by the 'massive changes' that have taken place. It is a 'one-sided' approach and not a 'comprehensive' approach. It is a 'one-sided' approach based on the aggrieved 'South' due to 'super-exploitation' by the 'North' and the 'legacy' of Imperialism especially the latter system of Imperialist colonization. The present 'map' of Africa was drawn up by Imperialist powers in their interests not in the interests of the peoples of Africa. The 'nation states' of Africa, after the 'termination' (Soviet 'Marxism-Leninism' word) of the system of Imperialist colonization, which arose, is the product of that 'legacy'.

The SACP Theses do not address the 'growing trend of economic integration' on the continent of Africa. The Southern African Development Community is only one example of the growing trend of economic integration. So is the African Union (AU) which is trying to copy the European Union without emphasis on the 'economics' of this 'development'. This 'surprised' me in my investigation of 'capitalist economic integration'. The SACP 'uses' the word 'integration' but nowhere does it discuss it scientifically especially in relation to Africa and based on Marx's 'second tendency' in the development of capitalism. The policy of 'financial liberalization', which includes 'Structural Adjustment Programmes', and that of 'good governance' in the stage of Globalization, demanded by finance capital and the monopolies or 'transnational corporations' (SACP words) of the 'advanced capitalist countries' of the 'North' is a means of the 'integration' of 'developing countries' into the global capitalist economy. One of the resulting factors is the 'breakdown of national barriers', which meant that 'developing countries' had to 'open-up' their economies, allowing 'foreign capital' from the 'advanced capitalist countries' to penetrate and 'super-exploit' the economies of the 'developing countries' in order to further 'capital accumulation'.

I digress slightly and would like to present at this 'juncture' the views of bourgeois ideologists on the 'behavior' of finance capital and their understanding of a 'global bank'. Berger, Dai, Ongena and Smith argue, in their article on the World Bank Website on Globalization, May 2002 titled "To What Extent will the Banking Industry be globalised? A Study of Bank Nationality and Reach in 20 European Nations", that a 'global bank operates in many nations and is among the world's largest institutions'. They talk that 'global banks headquartered in a few financial centers, but with offices in many nations around the world' have achieved their position through 'purchases of equity shares in foreign banks'. Furthermore, they argue that: 'These studies found that banks take equity shares in foreign banks in nations where economic growth rates are high…Banks that take equity stakes in foreign banks tend to be relatively large, profitable, and from nations with more developed banking markets.'

It is clear that through the 'force of attraction' and 'the tendency to centralisation' that finance capital or the 'global bank' from 'developed banking markets' or the 'advanced capitalist countries' are for the 'breakdown of national barriers' as this furthers 'capital accumulation'. This 'fact' is a reflection of the 'second tendency' in the development of capitalism (Marx) and described by the General Secretary of the Communist Party of Britain, Rob Griffiths.

Moreover, the 'global bank' is an expression of the 'centralization' of capital world-wide that Marx talked about in his work, *Capital*. 'Marxism-Leninism' is 'silent' on this side of the matter. The SACP talks about the 'massive changes that have taken place...' This is one of the 'massive changes' and the SACP is 'silent' on this 'change' which expresses the relationship between the 'global bank' and 'centralization' of capital in the former pursuit of 'capital accumulation'. Both, the bourgeois ideologists, Berger *et al* and the 'Marxist-Leninist' organizations like the SACP and the CPB, through their leadership of Blade Nzimande and Jeremy Cronin and Rob Griffiths, show themselves to be clueless on this 'quantitative and qualitative development and growth' of finance capital into 'global banks', dominating many nations especially in the 'South', (SACP word) and the 'centralization of capitals' (Marx) that is taking place. This 'development and growth' of 'centralization' of finance capital in the form of 'global banks' is not an expression of Imperialism but of 'mature monopoly capitalism' (Griffiths words) in the stage of Globalization. In the case of the bourgeois ideologists Berger *et al*, it is understandable that they are not aware of Marx's concept of 'centralization' as they do not adhere to the principles of Scientific Socialism. In the case of the leadership of the SACP and the CPB, their 'lack of awareness' of Marx's concept of 'centralization' is unforgiveable.

Rob Griffiths, the General Secretary of the Communist Party of Britain, shows a 'textual' understanding of Marx's 'two conflicting tendencies in the development of capitalism' because he does not subject it to an empirical investigation based on, for example, the European Union, where he will discover that there has been a 'breakdown [of] national barriers'. He does not develop 'revolutionary theory' based on Marx 'second tendency' in the development of capitalism. He, and his organization, the Communist Party of Britain, take a myopic view of 'mature monopoly capitalism' by looking at the European Union through the prism of 'Imperialism' and calling for 'withdrawal' from the 'Bosses Club' because it is 'undemocratic'.

'Mature monopoly capitalism' is showing that this 'second tendency' that Marx talked about prevails in economic life and is premised on the full application of the General Law of Capitalist Accumulation especially 'centralization' in furthering 'capital accumulation'.

'Mature monopoly capitalism' tendency to 'breakdown national barriers' shows itself in the European Union, North America Free Trade Area (NAFTA), and ASEAN, for examples. This is a very important development.

This 'development' or 'second tendency' in the 'development of capitalism' cannot be 'sited' in Lenin's theory of Imperialism. This was why an 'anti-imperialist approach' could not be taken. This 'objective fact' had to be sited in the *stage* of 'Globalization'.

It means that the propositional-statement 'Globalization is Imperialism' cannot be sustained. Faced with these 'global realities' (SACP words) the propositional-statement 'Globalization is Imperialism' cannot be held.

It was such 'massive changes' that led me to change my 'world-view' that 'Globalization is Imperialism'. It led me to the conclusion that 'Globalization' is the new, second, higher, and final stage of 'mature monopoly capitalism'.

'In the final analysis', 'centralization' has come to the fore. This 'particular' feature of the General Law of Capitalist Accumulation can no longer be restricted to 'theoretical' discussion. 'Centralization' is a fact of economic life within 'mature monopoly capitalism' in the second decade of the twenty first century. 'Marxism-Leninism' in general does not discuss 'centralization' scientifically. This 'ideology' is practically 'silent' on the matter in the second decade of the twenty first century. This can be clearly seen in the case of the SACP Theses and also through the CPB materials on its website. Soviet 'Marxism-Leninism', from the past, only discussed 'centralization' from a 'theoretical' side from the books that I have read. The 'emphasis' by them was on 'concentration of production and capital' with regards to 'state monopoly capitalism'.

I gave in the main body on the essay on Globalization a quote by Lenin from a 'Soviet' text-book of his criticism of those who talked about 'ultra-imperialism' like Kautsky, who linked 'centralization' to Imperialism. The notion of 'ultra-imperialism' is inappropriate for analyzing mature monopoly capitalism because the 'tendency to centralization' cannot be grounded in Imperialism given that it, Imperialism, is characterized with 'rivalries' and 'contradictions'. Therein lay the problem.

Nevertheless, 'centralization' prevails. This can be seen in the European Union and its central bank, the European Central bank' which is an expression of, to use Lenin's words, 'amalgamation of national finance capitals...' The European Central Bank (ECB) has developed through the process of capitalist economic integration that Europe has embarked on for over fifty years.

I came to the conclusion that 'state monopoly capitalism' (Lenin's concept) or 'mature monopoly capitalism' (Griffiths words) is 'engaged' (SACP word) with 'centralization' even though bourgeois ideologists and, especially 'Marxism-Leninism' do not understand this scientifically. In my investigations I was 'forced' to bring Marx's concept of 'centralization' back onto the fore front of the world political stage and within the context of 'Globalization' and not 'ultra-imperialism' nor Imperialism.

Centralization is one of those 'massive changes' that the SACP talks about that 'mature monopoly capitalism' has undergone in the last twenty-five years. Yet in their Theses on 'Globalization' the SACP leadership, represented by Nzimande and Cronin, are conspicuously 'silent' or they are clueless on the matter as Griffiths and the CPB are.

'Centralization' prevails, as I have shown', because 'state monopoly capitalism' is in the stage of Globalization.

I end by talking about the recent SACP discussion document (African Communist, issue 187, Fourth Quarter, December 2014) entitled "Going to the root - towards a radical, second phase of the NDR", in which they make comments on 'mature monopoly capitalism'. This is what they say:

"General global capitalist restructuring over the past three decades - involving increased trans-nationalization of operations, and, especially runaway financialisation. The latter a response to the crises of over-accumulation, falling rates of profits, and long-term stagnation in the developed capitalist core, has seen productive economy increasingly swamped by speculative financial activity (the global casino economy). This restructuring has resulted in the weakening of trade unions, growing inequality, the rolling back of the welfare state, and the unraveling of explicit or implicit social accords throughout the developed capitalist core." (p.17)

It is clear that 'General global capitalist restructuring of the past three decades' refers to a 'historical period', which I assume, given the SACP Theses, that it is a 'phase' of Imperialism. In 2014 we find the economic basis of this 'phase' of Imperialism known as 'Globalization'. It is 'crises of over-accumulation' and 'falling rates of profit' and more leading to 'runaway financialisation'. The 'Marxist-Leninist' SACP has slightly changed its position. In 2001, Cronin, one of its leaders and theoreticians, in his polemics with Mokaba, talked about 'crisis of accumulation', 'crisis of profitability' and 'swathes of loans' in order to explain the 'origins' of Globalization. Its present position is a slight improvement but it is insufficient and not scientific.

The SACP fails to see that the General Law of Capitalist Accumulation especially 'centralization' prevailing during this 'past three decades' of 'General global capitalist restructuring'. The SACP fails to see 'centralization' in the 'developed capitalist core' for example, the European Union. The SACP fails to see that, what it calls, 'runaway financialisation' is concerned with furthering 'capital accumulation' by finance capital and the financial oligarchy and is premised on the General Law of Capitalist Accumulation especially 'centralization'. Let us look at 'financialisation'. It is nothing else than the dominance of finance capital over all other forms of capital and is 'an enormous social mechanism' engaged in the 'centralization of capitals' (Marx)

I would like to provide, at this juncture, a quote from Simon Clarke's essay, published on the Internet, called *The Marxist Theory of Over-accumulation and Crisis* in which he talks about the 'general law':

"...and summarized in the 'general law' of capitalist accumulation, which expressed the contradiction between the tendency for capital to develop the productive forces without limit, on the one hand, and the tendency to restrict the consumption power of the mass of the population, by displacing living labour, forcing down the value of labour power and expanding the reserve army of labour, on the other hand." (p.6)

The above is quite a good summary of Marx's definition of the 'absolute general law of capitalist accumulation'. This has to be 'connected' to the 'deterioration in the lot of the working class' both in absolute and relative terms. This is a feature of the stage of Globalization world-wide which is not understood by the SACP and the CPB and is not an expression of Imperialism which Lenin grounded in 'concentration'.

The SACP fails to understand that one of the features of the General Law of Capitalist Accumulation, that of 'centralization', acted as a 'counteracting factor' to the 'law of the tendency of the rate of profit to fall' during the 'past three decades'. 'Centralization, expressed through both takeovers, mergers and acquisitions and through capitalist economic integration like the European Union, during the 'past three decades' re-invigorated 'mature monopoly capitalism' during this period of 'restructuring'. At the same time, there was the gradual deterioration in the lot of the working class especially in the 'developed capitalist core'. I repeat. The 'development and growth' (SACP words) of 'centralization' during the past three decades acted as a 'counteracting factor' in the' law of the tendency of the rate of profit to fall' and re-invigorated 'capital accumulation' especially in the 'developed capitalist core' and in relation to the boom period between 1998 and 2006 just before the Financial Crash of 2007/8.

Furthermore, (I am not engaged with the debate on the 'law of the tendency of the rate of profit to decline' and the 'counteracting tendencies') it has to be pointed to the SACP that 'falling rates of profits' or the 'law of the tendency of the rate of profit to decline' has its 'roots' in the General Law of Capitalist Accumulation, specifically, in the organic composition of capital and to the other features of it. It appears that the SACP leadership/theoreticians, Nzimande and Cronin, see 'falling rates of profits' but do not see the General Law of Capitalist Accumulation underpinning it. The 'connection' between the General Law of Capitalist Accumulation and the 'tendency of the rate of profit to decline' and its 'counteracting tendencies' within 'mature monopoly capitalism, in the stage of Globalization, in the second decade of the twenty first century, 'shows' that the 'general law' prevails.

The SACP fails to understand that 'crises of over-accumulation' have to be 'connected' to the General Law of Capitalist Accumulation. The 'general law' is the 'ground' for 'crises of over-accumulation' and yet it is not discussed by the SACP theoreticians, Nzimande and Cronin.

Recently, (April 2015) I visited the SACP website where they published the African

Communist and in it was an article by Masondo which is a contribution to the discussion document published by the SACP in December 2014 (which I have referred to above). This is his criticism of the leadership position:

"The GtR also argues that "global capitalist restructuring in the last three years was a response to the crises of over-accumulation, falling rates of profit and long-term stagnation. There is some element of truth in all three factors for capitalist restructuring. The GtR document only provides a hotchpotch theorization of global restructuring. Capitalist over-accumulation, stagnation and falling rates of profit are presented in an eclectic manner leaving the reader confused as to which of the three contains the underlying logic driving capital restructuring. As a result, it is difficult to distinguish theoretical categories of the surface and phenomena. The former does not capture what is the underlying logic of capitalism." (African Communist, 1st Quarter, 2015, p.64)

Masondo has not understood that 'Marxism-Leninism' has emphasized 'crises of over-accumulation' amongst other things as 'underlying' global capitalist restructuring. In my research and investigation, I found other 'Marxist-Leninist' parties taking this approach which is an analysis of 'capital restructuring' in this period that does not take in to account economic laws, for example, the General Law of Capitalist Accumulation, especially centralization. Masondo questions 'crises of over-accumulation' and which of the three is the 'determining element'. Masondo is correct that the position of the SACP leadership/theoreticians of Nzimande and Cronin is 'eclectic' and 'hotchpotch theorization'. He, however, fails to see the operation of the General Law of Capitalist Accumulation through its four features especially centralization during this period and in relation to the law of the 'tendency of the rate of profit to fall' and its 'counter-acting factors'. Masondo argues that profit is the basis of this period of 'capital restructuring'. In a sense, he is partially correct. It is not a question of profit. It is the question of 'capitalist accumulation' and the application/ relevancy of the 'General Law'. Masondo does not appreciate that it is very important to provide a scientific, law-governed analysis of this 'historical period' (three years or three decades is not clear) known as 'Globalization'. Both he and the SACP leadership/ theoreticians of Nzimande and Cronin fail to provide a scientific and law-governed analysis of this 'historical period' known as 'Globalization'. I have in this Conclusion argued that the SACP leadership/ theoreticians, Nzimande and Cronin do not develop their Theses on 'Globalization' on a *materialist* dialectic law-governed approach. I refrained earlier from calling their approach 'eclectic' and 'hotchpotch theorization'. I now have to agree with Masondo that their approach is 'eclectic' and 'hotchpotch theorization' especially in relation to its Theses on 'Globalization'.

The SACP, in this discussion document, talks about the 'High levels of monopoly concentration...' (p.14) but does not fully explain it. In the May issue 2016 of Umsebensi on the SACP website, in its May day Message, the SACP states:

"The degree of monopoly concentration in banking in South Africa is among the highest in the world - the four largest banks hold 84% of total banking."

This notion of 'monopoly concentration' might be applicable to South African monopoly capitalism but it is not fully commensurate with the behaviour of finance capital and the monopolies in the 'developed capitalist core' or 'advanced capitalist countries'. By talking about 'monopoly concentration' in South Africa the SACP fails to see the 'centralization of capitals' (Marx) that South African finance capital is 'engaged' (SACP word) with given that the SACP states that four big banks dominate the financial sector. The economy of South

African monopoly capitalism has occurring within it takeovers, mergers and acquisitions within the past ten years. These economic facts cannot be sited within the SACP notion of 'monopoly concentration'. It would be more appropriate to talk about 'monopoly concentration and centralization' rather than simply 'monopoly concentration'. I challenge the 'Marxist-Leninists' Nzimande and Cronin of the SACP to site takeovers, especially 'hostile takeovers' and mergers in monopoly concentration. The SACP does not see, is ignorant of, or does not understand Marx's very important concept 'centralization' when it develops the notion 'monopoly concentration' and treats it as an 'absolute'. This shows that the 'Marxist-Leninist' SACP treats Marx and his concept 'centralization' as a 'dead dog'. This is the reason why the SACP does not talk about Marx's main contradiction of capitalism that centralization of the means of production and the socialization of labour become incompatible with its capitalist integument especially in its Theses on 'Globalization' and with regards to the conditions of South African monopoly capitalism. The emphasis of viewing 'monopoly' through 'concentration' within South African monopoly capitalism and developing the notion 'monopoly concentration' narrows and limits its analysis. It elevates a *particular* feature of the General Law of Capitalist Accumulation to the level of an *absolute generality* to the conditions of South African finance and monopoly capitalism. The 'theoretical practice' of the SACP in analyzing South African monopoly capitalism is not only 'sloganeering' but also dogmatism The criticism, by myself, of the General Secretary of the Communist Party of Britain, Rob Griffiths, notion of '...concentration of economic resources...' also equally apply to the SACP notion 'monopoly concentration'.

I turn to the SACP notion 'trans-nationalization of operations'. What economic law or laws underpin this notion or phrase is not explained. The SACP leadership/theoreticians, Nzimande and Cronin have a 'habit' of 'engaging' in generalizations such as 'trans-nationalization of operations', 'runaway financialisation' and 'massive changes that have taken place'. It is also important for the 'advanced workers' to understand that 'trans-nationalization of operations' is a negation of Lenin's position of the economic and territorial 'division' of the world by the monopolies and the big capitalist powers. It becomes clearer when 'trans-nationalization' involves the breakdown of national barriers otherwise this form of capitalist economic activity cannot take place. I gave the very important quote by Stelzer in the essay on Globalization. In it he talks about '...Spain's Banco Santander snaps up Abbey...' This is a Spanish banking monopoly acquiring a British bank within the European Union. This can be called 'cross-border centralization' which leads to 'trans-nationalization of operations' due to the breakdown of national barriers.

In 2003 when I was investigating 'Globalization' there was Rob Griffiths '...concentration of economic resources...' In 2014 the 'Marxist-Leninist' South African Communist Party still clings to 'concentration' like Rob Griffiths except that they have developed the notion 'monopoly concentration'. It 'appears' (Hegelian concept) that 'Marxism-Leninism' still clings to 'concentration' and this 'shows' (Hegel) itself through its individual organizations like the South African Communist Party and the Communist Party of Britain. It appears that Nzimande and Cronin of the SACP have not understood the chapter on the 'General Law of Capitalist Accumulation'. The failure to see, the ignorance of, and the lack of understanding of Marx's very important concept 'centralization' shows the *dogmatism* of 'Marxism-Leninism'.

I cannot provide a detailed analysis of South African monopoly capitalism as this was not my objective. I can only make a few comments and this I have done especially in relation to the 'developed capitalist core' or the 'advanced capitalist countries'.

I 'hope' that the investigation on 'Globalization' gives 'food for thought' and discussion. I 'hope' that future discussion centers on Marx's main contradiction of capitalism and its relevancy or applicability to the European Union in the 'developed capitalist core' and in the 'developing countries' or the 'Third World' as it was called in my youth. Is the African Union an expression of the 'centralization' that is developing in the continent of Africa? Can this development of 'centralization', especially political centralization in the continent of Africa proceed on the basis of capitalism. The 'developing countries' especially South Africa, which is the most highly developed monopoly capitalist country in the continent of Africa, must come to an understanding of 'centralization' in order to create 'developmental programmes'. It is this development, from a personal point of view, that is going to be very important for the class struggle and the transformation to socialism.

'Mature monopoly capitalism', in the second decade of the twenty first century, in the stage of Globalization, has developed 'centralization' to such a high degree, to such a magnitude, that it is becoming a 'fetter' (Marx) and this is not being noticed or noted by the SACP and the CPB. This is not my 'understanding' but 'shows' itself in *practice,* for example, in Rob Griffiths '. concentration of economic resources...' and in the SACP notion 'monopoly concentration'. As Hegel remarked, I think, that *practice* is a criterion of truth.

Marx's main contradiction of capitalism 'shows' itself within 'mature monopoly capitalism', in the twenty first century, in the stage of Globalization, as one of the *objective* conditions for the transformation of capitalism into socialism. The 'problem' lies with the *subjective* factor, the communist organizations, which are indoctrinated by 'Marxism-Leninism', leading to 'dogmatism', which, in turn, leads to the stultifying of the political education and political consciousness of the working class, not only within the 'developed capitalist core' but also in the undeveloped and underdeveloped capitalist 'periphery', the 'developing countries'.

For myself, the SACP, in talking about the 'contradictions of Globalization' (read as Imperialism, given their 'sloganeering' [SACP cadres word] that 'Globalization is Imperialism') fails to mention Marx's main contradiction of capitalism in its Theses and this shows its 'dogmatism'. The SACP, in its Theses on Globalization, does not treat the very important concept 'Globalization' in a serious, scientific manner. The SACP 'Theses' is an abject and dogmatic *reaction* to bourgeois ideologists (read as 'neo-liberals) and 'vulgar Marxism' analysis of 'Globalization'.

Lenin pointed out that the working class has to be guided by the most advanced revolutionary theory in *What is to be done?* The failure to provide a serious, scientific and law-governed analysis of Globalization by the SACP, the CPB and by 'Marxism-Leninism' in general shows why the working class has not transformed 'mature monopoly capitalism' into socialism.

I did not envisage, when I started my investigation into the truth of the propositional statement 'Globalization is Imperialism' in 2001, that I would end up constructing a working definition of 'Globalization' as the new higher stage of 'mature monopoly capitalism'. The *"General global capitalist restructuring of the past three decades"* have resulted in the General Law of Capitalist Accumulation coming to the fore especially centralization, in both forms, necessitating a new higher stage of 'mature monopoly capitalism', that of Globalization. This was my surprise. Materialist philosophy, as developed by Karl Marx, has the element of surprise.

The second 'surprise' was the SACP contradiction of 'integration and marginalization of developing countries' and the CPB statement that that the '...EU is a creation of Western Europe big monopolies and is designed to serve their interests...' This is a *negation* of Lenin's position of the economic and territorial division of the world by the monopolies and the big capitalist powers. As I have stated it is not myself that shows that these features of the definition of Imperialism by Lenin provided by the SACP is no longer relevant to 'mature monopoly capitalism' but it is these 'Marxist-Leninist' organizations.

The third 'surprise' was in discovering the quote by Stelzer which proves the truth of Marx's concepts 'the force of attraction' and the 'tendency to centralization'.

The fourth 'surprise' was when Soviet 'Marxist-Leninism' theoreticians Rydina and colleagues (whom I have mentioned in the essay) have this to say on the General Law of Capitalist Accumulation:

"This law operates in all capitalist countries, but in different forms and degrees, depending on the specific historical conditions and the extent to which the working class and its allies are organised." ('Fundamentals of Political Economy' p.63)

In my investigation of the work of the above Soviet 'Marxist-Leninists', there arose a 'problematic'. It expressed itself when they argued that the 'General Law' operates 'in all capitalist countries' given the conditions, and at the same time argues that 'state monopoly capitalism' in the stage of Imperialism is premised on 'concentration of production and capital' (Lenin). The 'problematic' lies in the relation between the 'general' and the 'particular'. These Soviet 'Marxist-Leninists' cannot argue that the 'law operates in all capitalist countries' and at the same time 'absolutise' one particular feature of the 'law' that of 'concentration'.

It appears that the SACP is ignorant of Soviet 'Marxism-Leninism' position on the 'General Law' and its operation in 'all capitalist countries' because they make no mention of it in their publications especially on 'Globalization'. The SACP in its 2014 discussion document which I have mentioned above does not talk about the 'General Law' prevailing in South Africa's monopoly capitalism but only talks about 'monopoly concentration' and this is where it, the SACP, is not fully correct and is one-sided in its approach. The 'General Law' prevails within South Africa monopoly capitalism.

The same criticism applies to the General Secretary of the Communist Party of Britain and his 'absolutizing' of '. concentration of economic resources...' He does not see that the 'general law' fully prevails in British 'mature monopoly capitalism' especially 'centralization'.

The 'practice' of these two 'Marxist-Leninist' organizations, one from the 'North' and one from the 'South', in 'absolutizing' the particular feature 'concentration leads to the conclusion that 'Marxism-Leninism' is ignorant of the General Law of Capitalist Accumulation and dogmatically follows Lenin. 'Marxism-Leninism' cannot provide a scientific analysis of 'mature monopoly capitalism' because of its dogmatism and 'sloganeering'.

In the 'historical period' known as Globalization, the new higher stage of 'mature monopoly capitalism', the 'General Law' has acquired 'pronounced' significance especially centralization. The 'General Law', through its four features or 'particularities', concentration, centralization, organic composition of capital and the industrial reserve army which form different but connected 'moments' of this unity, especially centralization, leads to the deterioration in the lot of the working class, both in 'absolute' and 'relative' terms, which leads to the main contradiction of capitalism, which in turn leads to the SACP's contradiction 'the integration and marginalization of developing countries', generates 'crises of over-accumulation' and the 'law of the tendency of the rate of profit to decline', given the counteracting tendencies. These facts form different but connected 'moments' of the new higher stage of 'mature monopoly capitalism' known as Globalization.

I have, in providing a working definition of the stage of Globalization, emphasized Marx's main contradiction of capitalism which is connected to the 'General Law'. It was not of my choosing but 'forced' on myself through the economic facts. It was not my 'objective' or aim to bring back Marx's economic theory on capitalism when I first started to investigate the propositional statement of the SACP 'Globalization is Imperialism'. In the process of investigation, there were 'gaps' and 'silences' within 'Marxism-Leninism' especially in the analysis of 'Globalization' leading to 'dogmatism' and a one-sided approach. I was faced with 'Marxism-Leninism' emphasizing 'concentration' as the basis of 'mature monopoly capitalism' regarded as Imperialism, as is the case with the SACP with its notion of 'monopoly concentration', 'crises of over-accumulation' and 'falling rates of profit' and the CPB with its notion of '...concentration of economic resources...', whilst the economic facts showed that the General Law through its four features or particularities prevailed, especially centralization. I had to follow the economic facts, not the dogmatism of 'Marxism-Leninism'.

The final 'surprise', from a personal point of view, was that I 'became' capable of developing a theory of the stage of 'Globalization' based on the economic laws discovered by Karl Marx. I finish by quoting Soviet 'Marxism-Leninism' theoreticians Ryndina and colleagues whom I have mentioned above to show the myopic view and dogmatism of twenty first century 'Marxism-Leninism' especially the SACP and the CPB. This is what they stated:

"In the end, it is the accumulation of capital that brings the downfall of capitalism....

"The preparation and development of the objective and subjective prerequisites for the transition from capitalism to socialism are the sum and substance of the *historical trend of capitalist accumulation."* (pp66-67)

They finish by quoting Marx:

"With the advance of capitalism", Marx wrote, *"grows the mass of misery, oppression, slavery, degradation, exploitation; but with this too grows the revolt of the working class, a class always increasing in numbers and disciplined, united, organised by the very mechanism of the process of capitalist production. The monopoly of capital becomes a fetter upon the mode of production, which has sprung up and flourished along with, and under it. Centralization of the means of production and the socialization of labour at last reach a point where they become incompatible with their capitalist integument. This integument is burst asunder. The knell of capitalist private property sounds. The expropriators are expropriated."* (p.67)

It is clear that Marx main contradiction of capitalism prevails in the stage of Globalization. Centralization of the means of production in the hands of the 1% whilst 99% are living in poverty on a world-wide or global scale shows that this main contradiction prevails in the stage of Globalization. This 'monopoly of capital' is becoming a 'fetter'. This is one of the 'objective' facts or prerequisites in the transition to socialism. The working class can no longer tolerate the accumulation and monopoly of capital in the hands of the 1%. Socialism beckons. The subjective factor needs to be developed and politically educated to make the transition to socialism.

The investigation of 'Globalization' and on socialism revealed that 'Marxism-Leninism' does not have its roots in Scientific Socialism. 'Marxism-Leninism' has its roots in 'Stalinism' and in the period of 'developed socialism' in the Soviet Union became the dogmatic ideology of the International Communist Movement.

Soviet 'Marxism-Leninism' analysis of 'mature monopoly capitalism' which they regarded as Imperialism was premised on 'concentration of production and capital', following Lenin, is still being dogmatically followed by the SACP and the CPB amongst others. This position shows itself as insufficient ground for an analysis of Globalization.

The working class must reject and rebuff 'Marxism-Leninism' and embrace Scientific Socialism as the scientific ideology of the working class. This is especially clear on the SACP's treatment of the Scientific Socialist concept 'Globalization'. The position of 'Marxism-Leninism' in general on 'Globalization', on 'general global capitalist restructuring of the past three decades', and by its individual organizations like the SACP and the CPB must be rejected and rebuffed because they do not take into account Lenin's concept 'the creation of the international unity of capital' in the epoch of 'mature capitalism' both in economic and political terms.

With regards to the 'system of socialism' that Lenin discussed, 'Marxism-Leninism' must be rejected and rebuffed because of its espousal of 'state ownership' or 'public ownership' as the 'essence' of socialism and not the 'system of civilized co-operators', the co-operative system.

Scientific Socialism stands firm against such distortions by 'Marxist-Leninists' like Griffiths and Nzimande and Cronin on Globalization and the system of socialism. Scientific Socialism makes clear to dogmatic 'Marxism-Leninism' that the monopoly capitalism of Lenin's time differs from 'mature monopoly capitalism' of the second decade of the twenty first century and the 'massive changes' that have taking place must be analysed on the basis of a law-governed and comprehensive approach in order to educate the working class in the transition from capitalism to socialism.

----- END -----